The Little Bulbs

2

"Things as Helps Themselves"

The children next door came over this afternoon to ask for space for a garden. This happens every spring and fall, or whenever they see me planting something. I always allot a piece of ground, which they lay off neatly with a border of stones. Then they go about the business of digging and planting with great energy. They like little plants with little flowers—especially bulbs, because bulbs are easier to handle than seeds, or things with roots. Best of all are little bulbs with long names. Painfully and illegibly they print the names on plastic labels (which always get stepped on before the flower blooms). . . . *Anemone blanda* var. *atrocaerulea, Crocus tomasinianus, Chionodoxa luciliae.* . . . When I try to palm off bulbs that have been dug and need replanting, they say they want new bulbs out of bags with names on them, and nothing else will do. The planting goes ahead with enthusiasm, but once it is done the children lose all interest until they are moved to dig and plant again.

Gardeners of all ages, I find, are much more eager to plant flowers than to take care of them afterward. This must be the reason for the popularity of little bulbs. Once planted in a soil and situation that satisfy their requirements they can be forgotten until they begin to bloom. When we left Raleigh to come to Charlotte to live, there were bulbs in the old garden that had bloomed without any attention every year of the thirty-two years we had lived there, and had been blooming in it for a long time before we came. No flowers will ever be as beautiful to me as the crocuses and snowdrops I found there that first spring. When I saw their tips pushing up through a tangle of broken branches, old leaves, and dead weeds, I remembered reading in *The Secret Garden* by Frances Hodgson Burnett how that strange child, Mary Lennox, pushed open the gate of the secret garden and found sharp, pale points sticking up in the neglected flower beds, and whispered to herself: "They are tiny growing things, and they *might* be crocuses or snowdrops or daffodils." Later she said to the housemaid: "Do bulbs live a long time? Would they live years and years if no one helped them?" And the little maid replied: "They're things as helps themselves. That's why poor folk can afford to have 'em. If you don't trouble 'em, most of 'em'll work away underground for a lifetime an' spread out an' have little 'uns. There's a place in th' park woods here where there's snowdrops by the thousands. They're the prettiest sight in York-shire when th' spring comes. No one knows when they was first planted."

For bulbs to grow and increase in this untroubled way, time is needed, and space—especially if they are to spread by seeding themselves. When I asked Mr. Krip-pendorf which kinds are best for naturalizing, he wrote: "I have colonized daffodils by the millions, but the only bulbs that naturalize with me are things like scillas, chionodoxas, and eranthis. I have lots of self-sown snowdrops (*galanthus*), snowflakes (*leucojum*), *Scilla nutans,* and *S. campanulata,* and quite a few hybrids of *Anemone blanda* and *A. apennina* which I had planted close together. When I had a town house *Scilla sibirica* bloomed wonderfully in the garden. In April it looked like a blue sod. In the woods the leaves seem to smother them out. I suppose it is a question of getting the right spot. The other day I found a 'plantation' of *Scilla bi-folia* that had moved itself by seed for ten feet. Then I went to a bank where there are a lot of *Hyacinthus azureus*, and pushed away the leaves, and there were lots of spikes pushing through the ground, and thousands of green, hairlike seedlings. Crocuses would seed themselves if it were not for the mice—I always find a few clumps where they were never planted. But the only bulbs I have ever naturalized in a large way are the winter aconites. Last week I gathered and sowed sixty thousand seeds." When I wrote that I did not doubt the number of seeds planted, but did doubt his counting them, he replied that he had counted a thimbleful, and used the thimble as a measure for the rest.

In a small city garden, where little is undisturbed and plants are crowded together as closely as people, bulbs have little chance to seed themselves, and sometimes the seedlings are not even welcome. But wherever it is possible, even on a small scale, they should be allowed to grow and multiply in a natural sort of way; they should be encouraged to drift through odd corners, or spread themselves under shrubs and between the roots of trees. In Raleigh, where I had plenty of room, *Crocus tomasinianus* and *C. zonatus* seeded themselves up and down a long, shady walk in the most delightful manner, and a few dozen bulbs of *Muscari armeniacum* soon made pools of blue along the driveway. Even here in Charlotte, where there is less room, a few yards of space can be spared to *Cyclamen neapolitanum;* tubers planted three years ago are already producing myriads of tiny seedlings each fall.

"Things as Helps Themselves"

Some of the little bulbs show up best in mass, particularly those whose effects depend upon intensity of color rather than individuality of form. Others must be enjoyed one by one. Small flowers of precise pattern and undiminished beauty need pockets all to themselves in the rock garden. Or perhaps they need the sharp drainage and summer baking that a sunny wall affords, or the margin of a raised border.

I would like to have a little bulb blooming in my garden every day of the year, and I think it would be possible under favorable circumstances. December is the difficult month. Once, in Raleigh, I had a dark violet form of *Crocus asturicus* in bloom in the early part of December, but it did not persist. Another year *C. laevigatus* var. *fontenayi* bloomed about a week before Christmas. These can be replaced, and are cheap enough to allow frequent planting if they do not prove to be permanent.

Even in northern gardens bulbs carry the banner of bloom right on into the new year. In open winters I often read of a snowdrop in New England, or a crocus in the Brooklyn Botanic Garden, and Mr. Krippendorf says that nine years out of ten he finds an odd snowdrop in December. "I found a lonely snowdrop this morning," he wrote on the fifth of December, 1953. "Hellebores and a crocus (probably *C. longiflorus*) are also in bloom. Something has been in bloom every week in the year since January, 1952." Another year he wrote, on the nineteenth of November: "I just went out to see what I could see—only a few cyclamen, the double *Colchicum autumnale, Crocus zonatus,* and hellebore." In Virginia, Mr. Heath reports three forms of *Narcissus bulbocodium* in bloom in December, 1954: *N. foliosus, N. romieuxii,* and *N. B. tenuifolius.*

All this goes to show that the gardener who thinks the little bulbs bloom only in spring is missing the best of them. Rain lilies that bloom from frost to frost, cyclamen from July into November or later, colchicum and fall-flowering crocuses from August on into the fall and winter, and many other equally memorable performances await discovery.

3

Snowdrops and Snowflakes

Nearly everyone in the South calls a snowflake a snowdrop. No matter how often Southerners are told that *Leucojum aestivum,* found in every dooryard, is a snowflake, they go on calling it snowdrop, just as they go on calling camellias japonicas, and daffodils jonquils.

For no good reason the snowdrops (*galanthus*) are very uncommon in my part of the country—not that they will not grow, but because local gardeners think that in having leucojums they already have snowdrops.

I, of course, would like to grow every snowdrop I ever heard of. Although I started many years ago to make as complete a collection as possible, I still have only the common sorts, for many are rare and very hard to come by—and difficult to establish, as well.

When I asked Mr. Krippendorf about those in his woods he answered: "With me the Byzantine snowdrop is the earliest, blooming before Christmas. It has much wider leaves than *Galanthus elwesi*, which blooms in open weather in January. *G. nivalis* is the English snowdrop, with grasslike foliage. Usually it blooms in February or early March. This year the clumps were full of white buds in January, although they did not open until the middle of March. This has been an unusual season, as January was warmer than February or March. The English snowdrop is very rapid in increase, making good-sized clumps with dozens of flowers. I like the individual flowers of the broad-leaved varieties, but love the solid white clumps of *G. nivalis*. Have you ever noticed the delightful scent that snowdrops have?"

Mrs. Wilder had noticed it: "Earliest come the snowdrops, pale children of the snows, that carry within their frosted bells the first faint fragrance of the year. In sheltered places in my own garden they bloom early in February if not buried beneath heavy snow, and I have more than once known them to take advantage of an 'amazing interlude' of mild weather in January to slip out of the half-frozen muck and flower serenely."

Mr. Krippendorf occasionally writes of snowdrops at

Snowdrops and Snowflakes

Thanksgiving, and says that he rarely finds them later than Christmas week. But in 1945 he wrote on the twelfth of February: "Most of the snow has gone, except on the northern slopes, and last night was the first night since the snow came that it didn't freeze (down to thirty-three degrees, however). The ground is still frozen hard, but the snowdrops come up through the frozen earth under the snow. How do they do it? I looked everywhere on December the ninth, and found only the one that I sent you, so they must have grown through the frost. This is the first January since 1918 that I have not found any in bloom."

In Charlotte, I have found the Byzantine snowdrop in Mrs. Church's garden early in November, and when the weather is not too bad it blooms on through Christmas and into spring. Hers is an old planting in the light shade of deciduous trees on a western slope. The original bulbs, a dozen or so, have prospered and increased, and myriads of seedlings have come up among the rocks and in the grass nearby, spreading in wider and wider circles. In the tender winter sunlight they seem as frail as frost, and so do the slight sprays of the autumn-flowering cherry swaying above them. *G. byzantinus* bloomed in Mrs. Wilder's garden in December or January in good seasons, but sometimes not until February. And I have read somewhere of its blooming in Lincoln, Massachusetts, in January. This snowdrop is a natural hybrid between *G. elwesi* and *G. plicatus*, collected near Broussa in 1893. For some reason it has always been very scarce, and having lost my original stock I have never been able to replace it.

G. elwesi is not at all scarce, but the bulbs available are not always the best form and, as it is a variable species, the size and earliness of the flowers depend upon the variety. With me it blooms in January in an average winter, and I have even found flowers before the new year. Since there is such a difference of opinion as to its culture, it must matter little whether the bulbs are planted in full sun or part shade, but they do require a rich soil that is well drained and not too dry.

In parts of England, where the common snowdrops are in bloom by the second of February, they are called Candlemas bells.

> *The snowdrop in purest white arraie*
> *First rears her head on Candlemas Day.*

This day, the Feast of the Purification, is set aside for blessing the altar candles and burning the Christmas greens—a fitting date to mark the end of winter and the beginning of spring. In America this date is better known as Groundhog Day, when the little animal traditionally comes out of his hole, and if he sees his shadow —which he nearly always does—goes back in, bringing on six more weeks of bad weather.

G. nivalis, "the first pale flower of the unripened year," has its pet name wherever it is grown: *perce-neige* in France, foolish maids in Holland, snowbells in the Scandinavian countries, *Schneetropfen* in Germany, and, everywhere, fair maids of February, a name that it shares with nearly every frail early flower. And since its range is so wide, from the Pyrenees to the Caucasus, the winged flower with its heart-shaped seal of green varies greatly in its season of bloom and in its size and shape. One of the best is the noble variety *imperati,* the large-flowered and broad-leaved Neapolitan snowdrop, which grows in the hills near Genoa and Naples and has been prized by gardeners since the time of Clusius. Although a Southerner itself, it bloomed in my garden only one season before disappearing for good, and I am still seeking to replace it. The variety *Scharlokii* is the one that I have found most dependable. It prospered for more than a decade in a low, damp part of my rock garden in Raleigh. It is not the most spectacular form, but the small, drooping, green-tipped flowers come very early, often in late January. There is a variety *flavescens* with yellow marks on the inner segments, and even a double form. "I walked around the woods for hours this afternoon," Mr. Krippendorf wrote on the thirteenth of April, "and found the first jonquil in bloom. When I came in, Mary said she had never seen a double snow-drop, and so I had to go back to get her one. They are clumsy things." But there must be lots of people who like double snowdrops, for it is one of the forms that is nearly always available.

The European snowdrop is a woodlander that likes cool soil in damp, shady parts of the garden, but it has lots of Mediterranean relatives that require full sun and sharp drainage, although they like moisture at the roots. I suppose there is no use in coveting these rarities which never appear on American lists—still, you never know when things will turn up. There is one trio from the Greek mountains that blooms in the fall. The variety *elsae* is the earliest, and is said to have bloomed in September in England. This is from Mount Athos. *Rachelae,* of Mount Hymettus, comes next, followed by *olgae* (named for Queen Olga) from Mount Taygetus.

The great Crimean snowdrop, *G. plicatus,* is seldom listed. I came across it once, but procrastinated, and when I did order it, it was no longer to be had. It is said to have been the first flower to greet the eyes of the British soldiers when the snow melted after the long winter of the Crimean War. I doubt that many of them gave much thought to snowdrops, but one officer, a Captain Adlington, thought enough of them to bring bulbs home with him. "Mrs. Adlington of Bradenham, near Swaffham, Norfolk, gave bulbs to Mrs. Groom of Warham, Norfolk," Beatrix Stanley wrote in the *New Silva and Flora* (April, 1939). "Mrs. Groom gave some of the bulbs to her cowherd's wife, Mrs. Buttle, in whose garden they grew well. The Reverend Charles T. Digby, rector of Warham, sent blooms of it to Mr. E. A. Bowles in 1916. He and others, among them myself, acquired bulbs from Mrs. Buttle. It is a very fine snowdrop, and increases rapidly. From the two dozen original bulbs I now have several hundred. It is said to require more sun than other snowdrops, but here it does equally well in sun or shade." *G. plicatus* is one of the late bloomers, with large flowers, very round in bud, and wide leaves folded back at the margins.

I have had one other species, *G. latifolius,* from the Caucasus, which never even bloomed, although it is considered an easy one to grow. Coming from alpine meadows, it probably doesn't like the South, but I should like to try it again, for it is a late-flowering snowdrop and valuable on that account.

The snowdrop season is a long one. One year when Mr. Krippendorf wrote of finding the first one in November, he was still singing their praise on the sixteenth of April: "The late snowdrops (*G. nivalis*) are all gone, but the large early ones still look pretty good. I had not remembered that they are so much more durable than the late ones." But a five-month season is not accomplished in a day. It is the work of a lifetime.

Leucojum

The generic name of the snowflake, *leucojum,* is from the Greek. It means white violet, and was given to the plant because of the fragrance of the flowers. I never knew that they were fragrant until I read it in a book. The perfume is so subtle that you must warm the flowers in your hand before you become aware of it. If you trust in names there is a snowflake for each season— winter, summer, autumn, spring—but, like so many ideas that are charming in the abstract, the naming does not work out so well. The winter snowflake, *Leucojum hyemale,* blooms in spring; the summer snowflake, *L. aestivum,* often blooms in winter in these parts; and the autumn snowflake, *L. autumnale,* blooms in summer.

The spring snowflake, *L. vernum,* does bloom at that season—a month later than the galanthus, according to the books, but at the same time according to my garden record. The tips of the buds, folded between the leaves, appear above ground early in January, but they wait until the end of February to bloom. I keep hoping that a mild season will bring them out much sooner, but we have had none of our summer-seeming winters since Mr. Krippendorf dug clumps from his woods and sent them to me. I know of only one way to come into possession of the spring snowflake, and that is to be a friend of Mr. Krippendorf. Although this species has been common in British gardens since it was brought to England from central Europe at the end of the sixteenth century, it is very rare in America. In fifteen years of ordering *L. vernum* whenever I saw the name in a catalogue, the bulbs invariably proved to be *L. aestivum* when they arrived. The summer snowflake is the so-called snowdrop of southern dooryards, an indispensable bulb in gardens, blooming in February (or sometimes in January) and often continuing through April. But this robust plant, with lush foliage and a spray of little bells at the top of the tall scapes, is out of scale with the early rock plants.

L. vernum is called St. Agnes' flower in honor of the patron saint of young virgins. The modest, chaste, and solitary bells are wonderfully fragrant, but the fragrance is not of violets. It is of vanilla and of something else, something that eludes analysis. The buds swell when they are ready to open, but the lime-green tips of the petals remain tightly twisted into a point until they suddenly flare apart. The scapes continue to stretch up after the flowers open, and so, in a single clump, the nodding bells are hung on stems of varying heights, from one to six or more inches. The thin, polished leaves come with the flowers but develop more slowly. They are curved in a way that repeats the hooked flower pedicel in a delightful and characteristic rhythm.

Although in the type there is only one flower to a scape, there may be two or more in the varieties. In the variety *carpathicum* from the Carpathian Mountains the petals are tipped with yellow. The variety *vagneri* is a more robust form, said to bloom in January.

The bulbs Mr. Krippendorf sent me were increasing and blooming well in the leafy shade of the rock garden when we left Raleigh. I have read that they grow best in a soil that has lime in it, and it is recommended that they be planted four inches deep in a rich, moist loam.

The small-flowered, narrow-leaved species of leucojum, once a separate genus named for Acis, a Sicilian shepherd, are very different from the hardy spring and summer snowflakes. They are for mild climates only and even there need warmth and shelter, and must be kept as dry as possible while dormant. The soil should be a well-drained, sandy loam. I would like to try them all in North Carolina, but so far I have been able to acquire only *L. autumnale.*

The rare Mentone or winter snowflake, *L. hyemale,* also called April snowflake, belongs to the French Riviera where it is found on rocky cliffs near the sea. This and the triangular-leaved snowflake, *L. trichophyllum,* bloom in April. The last is a tiny native of Spain, Portugal, and Morocco, which has been in cultivation since 1820. The drooping bells, stained with rose color at the base, are in pairs.

L. autumnale, found on dry, sandy hills on both sides of the Mediterranean, is a choice bulb that has been treasured by gardeners since the early seventeenth century. I think that next to *Narcissus juncifolius* it is the most adorable little bulb that I know. The flowers are minute crystalline bells, one or two to a six-inch scape, hung on hairlike pedicels. As near as I can tell they are scentless. The scapes and pedicels are a dark wine color and there is a vinaceous tinge on the reverse of the segments. This species usually blooms in July in North Carolina, but when the spring is slow the flowers may not appear until the first of August. Or perhaps it is the amount of rain that determines their season. Like the rain lilies, they bloom at intervals, and after showers. The leaves follow the flowers and remain all winter untouched by frost. They are as fine as the new foliage of wild onions and therefore likely to be weeded out if you are not very careful to remember where they are. You must be careful to watch for the buds, too, when they spring up from the ground in midsummer. I once came very near snipping them off as I went along the path with the shears, trimming the thyme, and thinking not at all of what might be coming up from beneath. The leaves die away sometime in early summer, and this is the time to set out the bulbs, although I have planted them in fall with good results. They can be planted in summer as late as July, but then they will not bloom until the end of September.

L. roseum, also autumnal, comes from the hills of Corsica. The small, solitary flowers are rose colored.

4

Squills and Daffodils

All the daffodils
Are blowing and the bright blue squills. . . .
Amy Lowell, *Patterns*

At some time in early spring—it is hard to say when, for
each season has its own moments of crescendo and di-
minuendo—the gold and amethyst of aconite and crocus
merge gradually and imperceptibly into the yellow and
blue of squills and daffodils, and these in time give
"place to pillared roses, and to asters, and to snow."

Squills and Daffodils

Squills

The delightful thing about squills is that they are so blue, and the most intense blues of all are found in the flowers of *Scilla sibirica* and *S. bifolia,* those two tiny ones that bloom so early in the year and look so brilliant against the rain-darkened earth. "These species," Mrs. Loudon says, "I have now seen in flower every spring for the last ten years in our little garden in Bayswater, without the slightest attention being paid to them, further than restraining the different gardeners we have had from cutting away their leaves." It seems that the nineteenth-century gardener was much the same as the twentieth-century yardman.

The flowers of the Siberian squill, *S. sibirica,* almost match the pure blue violet in the Ridgway color chart, but there is a faint underlying tinge of rose on the inside. The penetrating blueness of the petals is heightened by the blueness of the anthers. There are from one to three small, nodding flowers on short reddish stems, appearing in late February or early March. The varieties bloom earlier. Spring Beauty is the first. It has been out as early as the twentieth of January, although in some seasons it is a month later. Mr. Krippendorf has found it in bloom early in February. The bud is the first part to show above ground, and I am always startled to find the first one lying on the leafmold like a piece of blue glass. Spring Beauty is the most robust form of all.

Six or more stout scapes, with flowers that are larger and of a deeper blue than those of the type, spring up from a single bulb. The variety *taurica* has bloomed in my garden for many seasons, at the earliest during the first part of February, and at the latest the end of March. The flowers are Windsor blue, a clear, pure tint that has no trace of violet in it. The dark blue hairline in the center of each segment is especially distinct in this form. There is also a variety *alba*.

Two plants are in the trade as *S. bifolia*. I cannot tell whether they are merely forms of the same species, or whether another squill is distributed under this name. It does not really matter from the gardener's point of view, for both are charming, but I like to get things straight. Both have a pair of gray-green leaves and sometimes a smaller third leaf. The spikes of one have twenty or more small, narrow-petaled flowers of cornflower blue, and those of the other have a few larger, white-centered flowers of a deeper, more intense color. Both are about six inches tall, and bloom at the end of February or a little later. *S. bifolia* comes from shady groves and sandy fields in Austria and Germany, and makes itself at home in the garden in either sun or shade.

Blooming at the same time as these small and early squills is a more robust species introduced from northern Iran in 1931 as *S. tubergeniana*. It is related to *S. sibirica*, but the flowers are larger and paler and rather more like puschkinias, with the same spicy aroma of woods in early spring. They come out looking as if they had been dipped in bluing, and with a sort of cold purity from having blue anthers and no trace of yellow. They grow paler with age, and the final effect is white. The flowers open at ground level, and as they mature the threadlike scapes keep pushing up until they are four inches or more tall, several spikes crowding up from each bulb. The stout, short, pale green leaves arrive at the same time. This squill is still comparatively expensive, but, even so, a very desirable early bulb.

The squill called star hyacinth, *S. amoena* (once called *Hyacinthus stellaris*, the starry jacinth of Constantinople), was sent to England in 1600 by Edward Lord Zouch, "a great patron of everything connected with flowers." For some reason this species is not popular with modern gardeners, and I do not remember ever having seen it listed. I have long coveted it, however, so let me know if you find a source.

These small and early species, none of them over six inches tall, are followed when spring is at its height by the English and Spanish squills, or bluebells. The common English bluebell, *Scilla nonscripta*, blooms unromantically in my garden sometime in April. I always like to have a few in the rock garden, but they are beautiful only when planted in such quantities as to seem a sheet of color; individually they appear to me undesirable in all of the forms. The horticultural varieties are many, and their names are alluring, but they are insignificant and colorless. In England the bluebell is commonly called the harebell, because, as Mrs. Loudon explains, the tremulous flowers are so delicately attached to their stems that they are stirred by the breathing of the hare "which always makes its cover in the tangled brake of the thick woods and coppices where harebell is found wild."

The stately Spanish bluebell has been grown in the South for so long that it is found in all old gardens. It is much too large for planting in the pockets of the rock garden where small flowers grow, but it can be used in its many fine forms in the outskirts of any collection of shade-loving plants. In England S. *hispanica* (usually listed as S. *campanulata*) was in Elizabethan gardens, and in America it was in the gardens of the early colonists. There are many garden forms. One of the loveliest came to me from Mr. Krippendorf. Spikes of large flowers of wistaria-blue rise to twenty inches. A white variety that I have had for a long time is small and close to the ground. It blooms very freely, at the end of March or a little later.

Mrs. Loudon said that the meadow squill, S. *pratensis*, blooms in June, after the spring-flowering scillas and before the fall-flowering ones. Here in North Carolina it blooms in mid-April with the English and Spanish bluebells. It needs a sandy soil in full sun and is one of the most satisfactory kinds for bloom and increase. It flowers in a blue-gray mist that lasts for three weeks. The meadow squill was brought to gardens from Dalmatia more than a hundred years ago, and from the same country comes the recently introduced S. *amethystina*. The new squill is much like the old one, but the scapes are twice as tall, reaching sixteen inches before they fade. The brittle flower spikes are like little glass trees of iridescent blue; rose tinted in the wide-open flowers, green tipped in the buds. They are not amethyst. I often think that the men who name flowers must all be color blind. Last year this lovely and late scilla bloomed with the Atamasco lilies (zephyranthes) at the very end of April. But it was a late season, and the bulbs were newly planted, so they may come earlier when they are well established.

S. *italica* is reported as the last of the spring-flowering squills, and also as one of the early ones. It bloomed for me but once, and that was in late April. It is not offered often, so I have not been able to try it again. Like the meadow squill, it must not be planted in the open, but in a sheltered place in poor, dry soil, and even then, Mrs. Loudon said regretfully, "It seldom thrives in small gardens." It is native to the Alps in that part of southern Europe where France and Italy and Switzerland come together, and was sent to England from these rocky pastures in 1605. The light lavender-blue flowers, on stalks less than ten inches tall, are scentless to me, although some say they smell like lilacs.

The season of squills need not end with the spring, for S. *chinensis* blooms in August. I first saw it in the rock garden at Cronamere, and was delighted with the feathery spikes of rose-colored flowers. Although it is easily propagated, the bulbs are seldom available, and it was only last summer that I managed to find a few. They came in July in pots and bloomed the first of August. The Chinese squill has been in cultivation for a long time and under many names. Mrs. Loudon knew it as Barnardia, a bulb sent from China in 1824 which made an "elegant appearance" in a pot, for she considered it too tender for the garden. This reputation seems undeserved. Mr. van Melle found the Chinese squill "of the easiest culture, completely hardy, and disposed to thrive wherever squills will grow, that is, in fairly rich, well-drained, loamy soil, and in a situation at least partly open to the sun in the flowering season, but protected from acute drying out in summer. Such a situation is often afforded by the foreground of a shrub border. We have found it a decidely worth-while and interesting plant in our Poughkeepsie garden, where it thrives lustily, increasing both from offsets and from self-sown seed, in a spot which receives only a few hours of sunlight on late summer days." [1]

The bulbs can be set out at any time, but spring or fall is preferable. I have planted S. *autumnalis* without success both in Raleigh and in Charlotte, but I can see no reason for this failure and shall try again when I can find another source (which is the real difficulty), for it is a plant "with no cultural fads . . . and remains, year after year, dainty and unassuming. The flowers on stiff little two- to three-inch stems begin to open in August

[1] *Bulletin of The American Rock Garden Society.* Vol. 4, No. 5, p. 85.

and continue well into October, and are thus a gentle reminder that it is high time that all those other bulbs, for spring bloom, were in the ground." I once had a little bulb—labeled *Leucojum roseum*—which it certainly was not—that bloomed charmingly in late summer, producing a spike of starry purple flowers that answered very well to the description of this squill.

"The thermometer is thirty degrees on the front porch," Mr. Krippendorf wrote one morning in mid-April, 1947. "While I was out I found *Narcissus diomedes minor* in bloom, also *N. gracilis.* I even found a puschkinia, the first for several years. I planted some of these bulbs before 1914, and they disappeared. But I keep finding them—just a few—far from the original planting. Of course I find seedlings of chionodoxa, scilla, and eranthis everywhere. And speaking of scillas, I was surprised to see that the white ones do come true from seed."

Puschkinia scilloides var. *libanotica,* the Lebanon squill, has come into bloom in my garden as early as the ninth of February and as late as the twenty-first of March, flowering with nemophila and *Hyacinthus azureus,* and looking very charming with them, for its pale bells are washed and delicately striped with the same pale blue. Not the least of their charms is the fine, spicy fragrance. I remember that the first time I had this little relative of the squills, I thought it rather unattractive. The few-flowered stems were only four inches at their tallest, and seemed to do most of their flowering underground. Later, Mr. Krippendorf sent me a fine form with larger, bluer flowers, nine to an eight-inch spike. These were as handsome as *Scilla campanulata.*

Little Daffodils

Many years ago, when I first began to collect little daffodils, I found that, however much the fact is deplored, gardening begins—and sometimes ends—in the armchair. You cannot grow little daffodils unless you have the bulbs, and difficult though their cultivation may be, their acquisition is sometimes more so. It must have been Mr. Moncure (or perhaps Violet Walker) who told me about Drew Sherrard. I wrote for a catalogue, and received a two-page leaflet entitled *Trowel and Typewriter.* Sandwiched in between lists of Oregon wild flowers and an announcement that Marion Hardy had finished "the delectable wild blackberry jam" and was now working with "big, fat, black huckleberries from the Cascade Mountains," were the following notes:

Little Daffodils: *Narcissus bulbocodium citrinus,* 15c; *N.b. conspicuus* 10c; *N.b. monophyllus,* 20c; *N. minor,* 50c; *N. nanus,* 35c; *N. triandrus albus,* 25c; *N. moschatus* (not more than 3 to a customer), 40c each; *N. canaliculatus,* 25c; *N. juncifolius,* 30c. Taking off the Latin masks, *bulbocodiums* are the hoop-petti-coat daffodils, *minor* and *nanus* are small editions of big trumpets, *triandrus* is the Angel's Tears, *moscha-tus* a white sunbonnet baby, and *canaliculatus* like a tiny Chinese lily. Three novelties that may win you a blue ribbon in next spring's show: *N. scaberulus* is the tiniest and rarest of all miniature daffodils, found only in one small valley in Portugal. These bloomed well here last spring; the cheerful little jonquil flower is only ½-inch in diameter. Only a few to sell at $3.00 each, and I believe I have all there are in the U.S. *N. watieri* is very little known as yet. It hails from the Atlas Mountains in Africa, and is an exquisite white starry flower with a shallow scalloped cup, or rather saucer, and gray-green foliage. Eight inches high, graceful and charming, $2.00 a bulb, and better speak quickly. *N. juncifolius rupicola*, a fine variety of the commoner *juncifolius*, with attractive bright yellow flower and flaring cup. Only a few of these, $1.00 each.

As I absorbed these provocative comments I pictured a small, sandy-haired gentleman in spectacles and a blue sweater, but when I fell into correspondence with their author (as was inevitable) I found that she was Mrs. Sherrard. "I plead not guilty to the blue sweater," she wrote, "although the spectacles are admitted. I never got around to figuring me out as a man, though when, as sometimes happens, I get a letter addressed to 'Gentlemen,' I do fancy us as an important group of rather paunchy directors around a mahogany table. As a Southerner, you are no doubt accustomed to the habit of giving girls as well as boys a family name as a Christian name. For instance, I went to school at St. Timothy's with a girl named Elliot Emerson. It seems to me she lived in Wilmington."

By the time I had worked through Drew Sherrard's list, and was ready to start all over again—with even more enthusiasm and perhaps a little more knowledge —on the ones that had failed, she wrote that she could no longer supply them, for World War II had commenced. "My garden is sadly run down," she said, "from lack of labor and my own preoccupation with other work. My only helper is an old man, a former North Dakota farmer. When he gets the shipyard bug I shall be at a loss to replace him."

It was not until some years after the war that miniature daffodils began to trickle back into the American trade, again to find their way into gardens. Now, of those that I longed for, all of these little members of the amaryllis family have bloomed in my garden—with the exception of *N. calicola* and *N. marvieri*. Every year new forms become available, extending the already lengthy daffodil season. The season begins with me before Christmas, with a little white petticoat, and lasts well through April. Of all the little bulbs, the flowers of these miniatures are the most endearingly diminutive, the most daintily perfect in proportion, and the most delicate in color. When they are in bloom I feel as if I could not stop looking at them for a moment, and when they are gone I am almost ashamed of the sharpness of my regret.

Most of the species can be brought to bloom by anyone who has a trowel, for they seldom fail to flower once, but keeping them is another matter. Gardeners in general regard them as transient. I once asked Mr. Krippendorf, who takes a long view of things, how long he was able to keep the very tiny ones. He replied that *N. triandrus* tarried only a year or so; that *N. minimus* seldom lasted longer although a seedling had once been found at least a thousand feet from the original planting; and that *N. juncifolius* does better: "It will keep on getting less and less for fifteen years before it finally disappears."

Billy Hunt, who gardens as Mr. Krippendorf does, in woodland and by the acre, gives an encouraging account of his plantings at Chapel Hill, North Carolina, where he says *N. cyclamineus* and *N. triandrus* have become established, and *N. minimus* grows like a weed. With me these come and go, although their going does not matter so much now that the bulbs are plentiful and cheap. By cheap, I mean that they are quoted by the dozen, not by the bulb. Now that I know they can be replaced I am not so frantic when they fail to reappear. However, Billy thinks they would stay with me if I dug a quantity of gravel from the garden paths into their soil.

Beginning with the small wild trumpets, there are *N. nanus*, *N. minor*, and *N. minimus*—small, smaller,

not a sturdy constitution. It bloomed one year in mid-March, and that was the last I saw of it.

Mr. Starker's *N. moschatus* lasted longer, at least four years, but bloomed only the first two seasons, in late February and early March. This had a longer stem, a drooping flower, and a crown longer and yellower than the segments. Also, it was fragrant.

The other two came from Mr. Heath. These were taller and larger than the ones I had had from Oregon, and both were the daffodils that I had already collected from old gardens. One is the daffodil known in the South as Silver Bells, and since it must have come from even older gardens in England I have often wondered if it were the same as those silver bells that Mistress Mary grew among the cockleshells, in what must have been an ancestor of the rock garden. I wondered, too, if her pretty maids were the Fair Maids of February (*Iris persica*) that grew with the Silver Bells in the same old gardens.

Mr. Heath wrote me that his Silver Bells came from Williamsburg, from a friend who said he had obtained them from England in 1910, and being "a most meticulous businessman finally unearthed the original invoice from Barr and Sons, London, with the name *moschatus.*" But now the English experts give the name of *moschatus* to another white daffodil, one which Mr. Heath imported from England in 1947 as *N. cernuus.* If *N. cernuus* becomes *N. moschatus,* the Silver Bells are again without a Latin name.

Squills and Daffodils

Peter Barr has written: "The botanists of the late eighteenth and early nineteenth century appear to have applied the name *moschatus* variously to the white trumpet daffodils known as *albicans, cernuus,* and *tortuosus.*" [2] This is borne out by William Baylor Hartland's description (in his *Little Book of Daffodils* for 1887) of *N. tortuosus minor* (*N. moschatus*) "as recently introduced from the Pyrenees; said to be Moschatus (musk-scented)? The blooms are all snow white, and varied in outline, gems for pots and rock work, and quite hardy; for gents' coats beautiful."

Mr. Krippendorf's solution to the problem of the white trumpets in old gardens is that they are all derived from a Pyrenean form, *N. pseudo-narcissus* var. *variiformis,* listed by Hartland as "a very free seed bearer." Mr. Krippendorf wrote: "If this form seeds freely and was sent out over the world, there must be countless forms scattered over the earth. And if you are trying to find names for them, you are sunk before you start, as they never had names."

With or without names the old white trumpets (with a few exceptions such as the dog-eared William Goldring which is really homely) are ravishing, and if small daffodils, not miniatures, are required they are to be regarded as highly desirable. We should be especially grateful to Mr. Heath for making two of the loveliest available.

[2] *Quarterly Bulletin of the Alpine Garden Society.* Vol. 3, No. 1, March, 1935, p. 67.

Usually the Silver Bells bloom very early, sometimes as early as the second week in February. In other years they do not ring out until March. The upright buds begin to dip as they open into the lovely swan's neck curve that is characteristic of many white trumpets. The flowers are what the old writers called dog-eared—the petals are twisted and swept forward as if blown by the wind. They are silvery at first but they fade to plum color—like Indian pipes. They are very much like Indian pipes with their bent heads and their look of unreality. Their crowns are slightly flaring and rolled back a little at the brim. They have a definite and individual fragrance, but whether it is of musk or not I cannot say, for I am not sure what sort of scent musk is. Mr. Heath's *N. cernuus*—or *moschatus* if you follow the experts, but I am not sure that I do—is also sweet-scented, but the scent is slight. This has a straight, narrow crown and slender pointed petals. The flower is smaller than that of the Silver Bells, and the stem shorter, but the neck is bent in the same way. This is sometimes called the silver swan's neck daffodil. It usually blooms the very first days of March.

Aside from these I have also found, in southern gardens, white trumpets with horizontally held flowers. One is about the size of *N. cernuus* with the same straight crown. Another, from Mrs. Harmon, at Saluda, South Carolina, is the smallest of all, and the last to bloom. At first, when they begin to bloom soon after the middle of March, the stems are short, but they lengthen as the flowers mature.

In modern gardens these old flowers are not always permanent, although they may have been brought from old plantings close at hand. This may be because the soil is too rich for them. They seem to thrive on neglect. "For white daffodils coarse stones," Mr. Hartland says, "or where the roots get in among the fibers of bush fruits, all the better; in such positions they will live and thrive for years and increase rapidly. Above all things, rank manure must be avoided."

Among the modern hybrids I have never found a small trumpet daffodil to my liking. Rockery Beauty is a pale, early, and not very small bicolor, blooming for me about the twelfth of March, and with Mr. Brumbach (in Pennsylvania), three weeks later. J. B. M. Camm, a very old variety introduced in 1884, is described as a midget with a five-inch stem, but it turned out to be a tall flower with a fine bold primrose trumpet and a pale papery perianth. Bambi, except for its earliness, which is a great asset (it sometimes blooms in early February), has no particular merit. It is a pale flower, not large enough to be striking, and not small enough to be charming. As to the white trumpets, I think nothing of J. P. Milner, or perhaps it does not do well in the South; and my only other one, Rockery White, has never bloomed. There are two really tiny yellow trumpets which I am looking forward to now that they are available, called Sneezy and Wee Bee, and a slightly larger one called Tanagra. Tanagra is a seedling of *N. obvallaris,* and has its parent's habit of rising early.

As near as I can tell there is no wild dwarf form of the large cupped daffodil, unless you count *N. macleayi,* a species of mysterious origin, which was sent from France to England in 1815 by Alexander MacLeay, and was grown by Mrs. Loudon in her little garden in Bayswater. "Mr. MacLeay's narcissus," she said, "is very distinct, from the breadth and greenness of the leaf, which in most *narcissi* is glaucous. The cup is fluted, and of deep yellow, while the limb is sulphur-colored." In modern times this species is, as Colonel Grey says, deplorably scarce. Mr. Krippendorf calls it *Diomedes minor,* Haworth's name. "If you like small things, I wish you might see *Diomedes minor,*" he wrote. "It is a charming thing and practically lost to cultivation."

Inevitably, the next spring I went to Ohio. It was past the middle of April when I left Charlotte and my garden in which there were irises and daylilies coming into bloom. It was such a sultry afternoon that I thought for a moment of leaving my coat behind. When the plane came down in Lexington, people were huddled in furs; and at Covington, small mean flakes of snow were flying. My heart sank as we drove through Cincinnati, where the only flower I saw was a shriveled bloom on an Oriental magnolia, and on through winter woods where there was no hint of green, and not a bud swelling. I could not believe that anything was in bloom any-

where, or would ever bloom again in that bleak coun-
tryside. Then Mr. Krippendorf turned the car into the
drive that leads to the house in Lob's Wood. There, as
if a door had opened into another world, was spring
spread out before me—a carpet of daffodils as far as I
could see.

Later, when we had searched the hillsides for *Diomedes minor*, and were about to give it up, I looked
down at my feet, and said, "What is *this* dear little
thing?" And there it was, just a few clumps among all
of those acres of daffodils, and yet so distinct that it
stood out from all the rest. Mrs. Loudon's description
is apt, for the foliage is arresting. The stiff, blunt leaves
are wide for such a small flower, and they have reached
their full height of eight or nine inches when the bud
opens. And so the flowers, on their three- or four-inch
stems, stand within the leaves, not hidden, but protected and shown to the best advantage. The oval overlapping petals are neither pure white nor exactly the
color of sulphur, but the tint that Ridgway calls sea-
foam yellow. The straight, narrow corona is creased
rather than fluted, in deep creases like accordion pleats.
The flowers have a certain stolidity and sturdiness in
spite of their small size.

N. macleayi soon found its way to my garden. "I
think you should help keep it alive," Mr. Krippendorf
said. It has now bloomed for four years (after taking a
year to become established), coming into flower about
a month earlier than it does in Ohio. This spring there

was bloom for three weeks, and the clumps have increased so well that I can begin to divide them.

Of the dwarf forms of large-cupped daffodils that are just beginning to be available in this country, I have had only Goldsithney, which sounds so charming but proved disappointing. Described as a tiny flower of vivid gold, it turned out to be a washed-out yellow, neither large nor small, neither early nor late, its charm only in its name. I still covet Mustard Seed (a miniature all in yellow), the orange-cupped Marionette, and the all-white Angie.

Three little small-cupped daffodils bloomed for me for the first time this spring. Two came at the end of March: Picador, a sturdy dwarf with round, overlapping ivory petals and a large flat crown of chrome yellow, and Xit, a replica of *N. watieri*, with the same sparkling whiteness and fine modeling, but with a longer stem and broad foliage. The third, Lady Bee, is dainty though not small, and has a shallow cup edged with pinkish buff. It bloomed early in April. Any daffodil blooming before or after March pleases me, but during March, when there are so many, I find myself more discriminating.

Parkinson called *N. triandrus* the turning jonquil because of its twisted stem—a better name than Herbert's, I think, for he named it for Ganymede, the cupbearer. The round shallow crown is very much like a cup but not very practical for bearing nectar, as it is upside down.

Squills and Daffodils

N. triandrus is cheap and plentiful, and, in spite of its reputation for being difficult, is one of the most popular of the little daffodils. I think that its popularity is mainly due to the sentimental name of the typical *N. t. albus,* which Peter Barr called Angel's Tears. The truth is (or so the story goes) that these tears were not celestial, but the very real ones of the native guide, Angelo, who wept from exhaustion when Mr. Barr (whom he was supposed to be leading) dragged him to a spot, high in the Asturian Mountains, where this little daffodil grows.

In my garden I replace it from time to time. Two or three frail flowers bloom on slender seven-inch stems about the middle of March. Mr. Brumbach says he has kept it eight years, and it blooms early in April. *N. triandrus* is a variable species with a number of fine forms. A very large snow-white one with flowers twice the size of those of the type is called *N. t. calathinus.* It is considered the most beautiful and the most difficult—attributes which seem often to go together—and I have never been able to bring it to bloom. The golden variety *aurantiacus* was not so deep a color as I expected, but a very fine flower that braved some nasty cold weather. The variety *pulchellus* is a bicolor, and *concolor* a pale yellow self. They all bloom about the same time, and all have translucent petals turned back from the smooth round cups. The threadlike foliage usually is scant.

"Have you J. T. Bennett-Poë in your garden?" Mr.

Krippendorf asked once in April. "If not, let me know, and I will say 'harkening and obedience'!" He sent me a clump in bloom, which has bloomed for me ever since, usually before the middle of March. I have never seen Bennett-Poë listed, nor met with it elsewhere, although Mr. Krippendorf has kept it for fifty years. A cross between *N. t. albus* and Emperor, it is a small milk-white trumpet in appearance, as sheer as Angel's Tears but not so tiny.

N. johnstoni, the Queen of Spain, another cross between *N. triandrus* and a trumpet, is a natural hybrid found in Spain and Portugal, which has been in cultivation since 1886. The straight, slender crown and the more or less reflexed petals are canary yellow, and of a firmer substance than those of Bennett-Poë. The flowers show a variety in form that is rather charming. Over a period of years they have bloomed in my garden as early as the fifth of March and as late as April Fool's Day. They do not grow well everywhere, and my garden is one that will not hold them very long, but they are well worth replacing.

Raindrop is the smallest and dearest of the recent *triandrus* hybrids, and also one of the latest. It blooms for me at the end of April, drawing out the already very long season. The three small flowers that hang in a row at the tip of the slender stem are as sheer and silvery as Angel's Tears, but with a substance that enables them to last in the garden for two weeks. Mr. Heath says Raindrop is worthy of a sonnet.

Squills and Daffodils

April Tears and Hawera are *triandrus-jonquilla* hybrids with the pallor and translucence of the *triandrus* group, the flowers being of the tenderest yellow. April Tears, one of the most floriferous as well as one of the smallest and most charming, blooms in my garden about the middle of April. Once a single bulb produced nine stems with two or three flowers to a stem. It is more appealing than Hawera, for the shorter stems suit the frailty of the flowers, but it is not so dependable. Hawera has bloomed faithfully for me, late in March, for a number of years. The clump is usually in bloom for at least three weeks, for the flowers are very long-lasting. They are as pale as moonlight and as delicate as frost, with a perfume that is like a cordial. The bulbs have not increased, as they are said to do, and I am wondering if the plant would be more robust in full sun than at the foot of a pine tree. The difficulty with all of these miniature hybrids is to know what is best for them, since so little has been written on the subject; thus they must be submitted to the trial-and-error method.

Three *triandrus* hybrids that have come to me recently are not so diminutive as Raindrop and April Tears, but they have the grace of the very small daffodils. There is an elfin quality in the tilt of the petals of Lemon Heart and in the poise of its crown. When it first comes out, on All Fools' Day or earlier, according to the season, the petals are straw-colored and the crown is a slightly deeper tone, but with age the whole flower fades to ivory white. The second of the three hybrids is Auburn, but except for its delicacy there is nothing about it to suggest *N. triandrus.* The petals are not reflexed, the fluted crown is narrow, and the color is the sparkling yellow of the jonquils. It blooms early in March. The third one, Kenellis, happened to be planted near *N. t. albus,* and bloomed at the same time. Seen together, their relationship is apparent, but Kenellis has traits of its own: the slender petals are not reflexed; in fact, they almost bend forward, and the pale citron crown is flaring. There is something of the charm of Bennett-Poë in the proportions and the hyaline quality of the flower. In Pennsylvania, Kenellis blooms in mid-April.

Frosty Morn has none of the delicacy of these three. Although it is dwarf in stature, the heavy substance of the twin flowers and the thickness of the stem in proportion to the flower size give it the sturdy appearance of a *tazetta.* However, if you are not expecting something else, the white flowers are very pretty, and they have the merit of blooming in April.

It seems strange to read that the cyclamen-flowered daffodil, *N. cyclamineus,* was known to Pierre Vallet in 1608. I never thought of Frenchmen of that day as concerning themselves with miniature daffodils. It is still a rare species, and not always accommodating, although it has become naturalized in some British gardens. I have planted bulbs a number of times, and still—like Mr. Brumbach—feel that I could keep them if I could only find the right place. The flowers appear here (if at all) the latter part of February, and in Pennsylvania early in March. The length of their narrow, cylindrical crowns is exaggerated, and the slender petals lie back against the stem, making the flowers look like fairy firecrackers. Their color is the palest spring yellow with a hint of green. I have always planted this species in damp shade, as it grows along streams in its native Portugal, and I have read that it likes shade. Now I think I shall try Billy Hunt's method of a bank and high shade.

Fortunately I have had more success with the *N. cyclamineus* hybrids than with the species. Mite, one of the most delightful, comes from Grant Mitsch in Oregon where it flowers late in February, as it does with me. It is a replica of the species, but three times as large. John Thibodeau writes that in Massachusetts it is very "prolific and rewarding, and it is not unusual for a good bulb to produce two or three bulbs in succession, thus prolonging the flowering season up to three weeks in cool weather." [3]

Another darling little one is Cyclataz, a wild hybrid between *N. cyclamineus* and Soleil d'Or. In spite of its background it has proved to be hardy in the New York-Philadelphia area, and perhaps farther north. With me it is thoroughly satisfactory, blooming between the middle of February and the first of March, producing on short, sturdy stems two or three flowers with the

[3] *Horticulture.* September, 1953, pp. 374-75.

warmth of the sun and the pallor of the moon in their golden crowns and citron petals. Unfortunately there is no trace of the *tazetta* fragrance. The flowers are not so fragile as they appear, for I have seen them unmarred by heavy frost.

The real miniature of this group—at least in the form that I have—is Minicycla, which is so small that I stepped on a bud twice while searching for it. It bloomed anyway, in the middle of March. The flower was like *N. cyclamineus,* but there must be some variation here, for the clump pictured in *Gardening Illustrated* (March, 1952) is more like its other parent, *N. asturiensis.* In a letter accompanying the picture, Maurice Amsler says: "My bulbs, few in number, were given me by Mr. James Platt, in whose garden at Chudleigh, in South Devon, many more of these hybrids had appeared during and after the last war. . . . Minicycla has many attributes apart from its very obvious charm. The flowers must be as tough as parchment, for the photograph was taken after they had been fully open for six weeks. The bulbs have that pleasing trick of increasing very quickly."

There are other dwarf daffodils among the *cyclamineus* hybrids, but to me the bold trumpets of Golden Cycle, Le Beau, and Peeping Tom, and even the daintier ones of February Gold and March Sunshine, are much too overgrown to be classed with the little bulbs. However, I must include Beryl, which has the form of its *poeticus* parent, but the shimmering petals are turned back from the small bright cup, and they are washed with the green gold of *N. cyclamineus.* This is a most satisfactory variety, growing well, flowering well, and increasing well in woodsy soil in part shade.

The rush-leaved daffodils, called jonquils from the Latin word *juncus* meaning rush, contribute most to the rock garden—especially in the South. They form a large group of miniature and dwarf species, and recently some delightful small hybrids have been produced.

I have been sitting at my desk for several mornings trying to make some sense of the descriptions of the little jonquils that grow in Spain and Portugal, and I have come to the conclusion that no two writers speak of the same flower under the same name, and so I shall describe the ones I have had, and let it go at that. I have grown two distinct forms under the name *N. juncifolius.* One I have had several times in Charlotte and in Raleigh, and it has never bloomed after the first year. It is a tiny replica of *N. jonquilla simplex,* with small round cup, flat perianth, the typical deep yellow jonquil color, and the typical round foliage and heady fragrance. The flowers put in an appearance in late March. The other one, which blooms in April at the very end of the daffodil season, answers to some descriptions of *N. rupicola.* The flowers are a clear, cool lemon color with a delicate precision about their modeling, a slight backward tilt of the petals, and an evenly scalloped and flaring cup. They have a faint but pervading perfume, like a long-unused spicebox. The leaves are narrow, gray, and flat. This delightful jonquil is still thriving in my garden (in spite of my having planted some fall crocuses on top of it) in rather poor, dry soil, in part shade, at the foot of a large pine tree.

An even smaller jonquil than either of these once bloomed for me, and I think it must have been Mrs. Sherrard's *N. scaberulus,* although I have no record of having acquired it. (One of the delightful and maddening things about gardens is the way strange things are always turning up, and you can never remember having planted them. One of the most beautiful little daffodils I ever had appeared in this way, bloomed for several years, and disappeared as mysteriously as it had come. Since the flowers were small and pure white I thought it might have come from Mrs. Sherrard as *N. watieri,* but she could not identify them as anything she had ever known.) The *N. scaberulus* bloomed at the end of March, and whether the true species or not, was certainly the smallest daffodil I have ever seen, or could imagine—a scrap only half an inch across, less than an inch tall, and with two minute leaves.

Mrs. Sherrard's *N. watieri* never bloomed for me, nor did the one I had from Mr. Robert Moncure, who grew it successfully in Virginia many years ago. Mrs. Sherrard sent me flowers in a letter, and they arrived in Raleigh as fresh as if they had just been picked, but I never had it in bloom myself until I came to Charlotte. Here, two plantings from separate sources are growing and blooming, one under a pine tree and one in the open on a low stone wall. The bulbs should be planted among flowers that do not have to be watered in summer, and where they will have a thorough baking, for they come from "sun-baked slopes and scattered woods of evergreen oaks." *N. watieri* is the only pure-white species of the jonquil group. Its habitat is in the Atlas Mountains, across the Mediterranean from the yellow-flowered jonquils of the Pyrenees. It begins to bloom early in March, and blooms for a long time—which seems to be characteristic of little jonquils. Just when you think they are gone for another year, a new bud appears. The silvery-white flowers have the same small-ness, purity, and perfection of design as the yellow forms, with a comparatively large, flaring, and evenly scalloped crown. The leaves are pale green, glaucous, very narrow but flat.

Except for *N. jonquilla* var. *minor*, these are, as far as I know, the only miniature species available in this country at present, although Mr. Heath promises two more tiny jonquils, *N. calcicola* and *N. marvieri*. The first is similar to *N. juncifolius*, only earlier in bloom and an inch or two taller. The other is like *N. watieri*, except for its yellow color, and is also a native of the Atlas Mountains.

N. jonquilla is said to have come to England from Spain in the reign of Queen Elizabeth and must have come to this country in the early days of the colonies, for there are numerous forms in old gardens, especially in South Carolina. One spring the earliest of these was in bloom in my garden on the twenty-sixth of February when I started to South Carolina in a snowstorm. The snow was so heavy that I thought for a while I would have to turn back, but by the time I got to Sumter it had become a thin rain, and every dooryard was filled with jonquils, the same type as the little one that I had left under the snow.

I asked about them and found that they had invariably come from other gardens, mostly old ones. This is a very distinct form in flower and in foliage, as well as in the earliness of the blooming season. The flowers come several to a stem and begin to bloom as soon as the scape pushes out of the ground. When they mature, the stems are about six inches long. The pale yellow segments curl inward at the edges, making a star-shaped flower with a bowl-shaped cup of a deeper color. It is a perfect rock-garden jonquil except that the foliage is very coarse. The curiously thick leaves are triangular at the base, tapering out to a very long, very thin point.

The next to bloom is the smallest and daintiest of these old garden forms. It is like the one I know as the var. *simplex,* only smaller in all its parts and with longer leaves. This blooms early in March and is followed by *N. j. simplex,* a charming affair with rat-tailed leaves and several heavily scented flowers on a ten-inch stem. Another coarser, taller, and later-blooming form is also given this name. A distinct jonquil that I have found in North Carolina gardens has very thick foliage and flowers with petals that stand out separately like the spokes of a wheel.

Gardeners who are lovers of old flowers often complain that whenever they order Queen Anne's jonquil they get the wrong plant. This is because two double daffodils are named for Queen Anne (not for the English queen, as I always supposed, but for Queen Anne of Austria). The one that has long been cherished in the South as Queen Anne's jonquil is *N. j. flore pleno.* My bulbs came to me from a commercial source, but I felt sure they were still to be found in old gardens although I could never trace them definitely.

At last a chance visitor told me about Mrs. Gibbs (née Le Conte). I wrote to ask her if she had the jonquil, if she knew anything of its history, and if she was related to Cousin Emma Furman who was also a Le Conte from Columbia. She replied that she had millions of the little Queen Ann's jonquil (with no nonsense about spelling Ann with the e), and that Cousin Emma was her favorite relative. "My mother knew the jonquils from her earliest childhood," she wrote, "and we have known of them from various places in South Carolina—always from an old Scotch ancestry. As far as we know our planting is the only one that has survived. It is at one of the old places belonging to my mother's side of the house, which was the home of my grandfather's old aunts, and he was born in 1812. Does your Queen Ann bloom every year? She is temperamental."

I couldn't answer this question very well, as I have

had this jonquil only two years. I have an idea that it is fugitive, but J. Jefferson-Brown writes in *Gardening Illustrated* (April, 1950) that it grows so well as "never to throw a bad flower." He describes it (with too little respect for its name, I think) as "a splendid fellow in the rock garden."

The reason that I have had Queen Anne's jonquil for such a short time is that I have an aversion for double flowers, especially daffodils. Mr. Krippendorf sent some to me, and I planted them without enthusiasm. When they bloomed, early in April, I had a change of heart. The flowers are as fragrant and as golden as the single forms of the jonquil, but with an added delicacy that makes them even more appealing.

Mr. Krippendorf also sent me specimens of what he called Queen Anne's double daffodil. "I ran across a few *N. eystettensis*," he wrote early in April. "It is quite a nice thing, but rather a weak grower. It has been under a beech tree for thirty-odd years." I had often wondered where this species got its name, and found in *Gardening Illustrated* (January, 1948) that it came from Basil Basler's *Hortus eystettensis* (1618), in which it was figured for the first time, although it had been mentioned by Lobel in 1581. Its origin is unknown (for it is not a double form of *N. capax*). Gerard had it from Jean Robin of Paris, but it is not known where Jean Robin got it. The curious flower has no crown—only numerous pale yellow petals arranged in even ranks to form a six-pointed star.

I may as well mention two other odd little daffodils before I go back to the jonquils. Both came from Mr. Heath. Kehelland is one of Mr. Alex Gray's new introductions. It bloomed the first year on St. Patrick's Day. The soft yellow flower has a rather long, narrow trumpet full of extra petals, and a single perianth. Pencrebar, named for the Cornish garden in which it was found, "like a soft yellow rose," as Mr. Heath says, blooms two weeks later. Neither of these blooms well for me.

One of the best of the dwarf jonquils in old gardens is Mr. Heath's Helena, which he found in Virginia. It blooms here with great profusion and regularity about the tenth of April. The flowers are chrome lemon, about an inch and a half across, of good substance, and very fragrant. They begin to bloom on five-inch stems but stretch up a little later on. There is nothing delicate about this one, but it is gay, dwarf, and dependable.

Mr. Heath offers a form of *N. jonquilla* which he calls var. *varicolor,* and describes as having variable straw-colored flowers. I have seen a similar one in Mrs. Lay's garden in Chapel Hill. She had a number of others, among them a dwarf and a very early one that was dug from the yard of an old house in Richlands, North Carolina, and is also to be found in Williamsburg. *N. j. citrinum* came from two sources. I can find no difference between either of these and the silver jonquil, *N. tenuior* (now considered a variety of *N. gracilis*), which usually blooms the latter part of March. It is very free-flowering and rapid in increase. The pale yellow flowers, an inch and a half across, come two or three to a stem, the stems only six or seven inches tall when the buds open. As the flowers mature they become silvery.

"A charming group of jonquil hybrids has been produced by crossing *N. juncifolius* with some of the garden varieties of *N. poeticus*," Alec Gray writes in *Gardening Illustrated* (August, 1946). "They flower when nearly all other daffodils are over and bear two or more showy flowers, yellow, with orange-red cups, on each stem. Lintie, La Belle, and Little Prince are the best, and flower in the order given. All are six to eight inches high."

Lintie bloomed for me on the eleventh of April, with two flowers (two and a half inches across) to a stem. The slightly tilted petals are a pale sulphur color with a shimmer of gold. On my specimens the rim of the flaring cup is not red but orange. Lintie has a subtle perfume instead of the intense fragrance of the jonquil parent. La Belle is very like Lintie except that the shorter stems make it even more charming. It has proved to be one of the most satisfactory dwarf varieties I have had. It usually blooms with Lintie, but is more variable. Comparing my dates with Mr. Brumbach's for the same season, an early one, I find La Belle coming into bloom in my garden on the fifth of April, and in his on the third of May. Mr. Brumbach finds that these hybrids of the jonquil, and various others that might be expected to be tender in Pennsylvania, are proving satisfactory. I think any difficulties are due more to lack of knowledge of their ways than to the climate.

I have had my troubles with Pease-blossom which bloomed once at the end of the season and never appeared again, and another little all-yellow one called Sun Disc, which never bloomed at all. Pease-blossom is not at all like a jonquil, but has the pallor, the fragile proportions, the rounded cup, and the winged petals of Angel's Tears. I shall try these two again in a sunnier spot. I must also have another tiny, all-yellow one called Yamlof.

The most delightful of all is Flomay. Its smallness and the silvery translucence of its petals make it the most appealing of the jonquils. Everything about it is little, the flower, the stem, the grassy leaves, everything except its fragrance; the characteristic jonquil perfume is overpowering in so small a flower. I have put the bulb in a safe place, between a stone of the garden steps and the base of a low wall, where it will be protected, and where I hope it will remain, for it is one that I would like to have with me always.

I cannot leave the jonquil group without mentioning *N. gracilis*, although it is much too tall and graceful to be called a little bulb. Still, it takes up little space and can be tucked away and forgotten until the pale, sweet flowers bloom. With me they last almost to the first of May, and Mrs. Wilder notes that they were often still in bloom at the end of May, rounding out her season which began with *N. minimus* late in March.

The dwarf of the *tazetta* group is *N. canaliculatus*, a perfect miniature polyanthus, with three or four crisp little flowers to a scape. The whiteness of the reflexed petals is in contrast with the deep yellow of the globular crown. The flowers have the heavy perfume that is characteristic of this group. Looking back over my notes I see that the blooming dates vary greatly. The earliest occurred this year, the twenty-second of February, and the latest the second of April—that was in Raleigh.

This daffodil comes from Mentone and likes a mild climate. Mr. Brumbach told me that he planted fifty bulbs in Pennsylvania without having a single flower. Mr. Krippendorf grows them in a frame. Here, they bloom very freely the first few years, but after that they are uncertain. The theory is that they require frequent division because they increase so rapidly. Otherwise this is an easy sort to grow in a sunny place where the soil is moist in spring but dry in summer. I rather believe that a summer baking is the important thing in getting them to bloom.

There is no really miniature poets' narcissus, but I like to have this group represented, and so include the slender *N. poeticus* var. *radiiflorus*, "a truly wild type of the Alps of Central Europe." The relatively small flowers are on tall, stiff stems like stilts. They have a green-gold sheen when they come out, but as they mature they become pure white. The petals all differ slightly in size and shape, and this irregularity is charming, as they stand out separately and tilt away from the small, red-rimmed cup. The foliage is tall and thin and stiff like the stems, so that the whole plant makes a vertical pattern that is characteristic and pleasing.

The hoopskirts are the best of all little daffodils for warm climates, but Mrs. Wilder noted that only two need concern the open garden north of Baltimore: *N. bulbocodium citrinus* and *N. b. conspicuus,* which bloom in her Westchester garden late in April or early in May. "These charming things," she adds, "are not difficult to grow; indeed with me they have proved the easiest of the little daffodils, asking only a gritty soil in partial shade and good drainage." Since Mrs. Wilder's gardening days many new forms have been introduced, and Mr. Brumbach, after trying them out at Reading, has added *N. b. romieuxi* and *N. b. obesus* to the hardy ones.

Forms of *N. bulbocodium* have been in cultivation in Europe since the sixteenth century, and must have come to this country in the early days, for they were in the original planting at Monticello. The flowers are entirely different from all others, with flaring crowns "distended as though drawn over a hoop," and small bractlike, green-striped petals. The leaves are round, dark, and shining like those of the jonquils but much shorter.

N. bulbocodium is widespread in the western Mediterranean region, with many forms that vary in their requirements according to their habitat. However, I find that the majority like full sun and good drainage, and are not particular beyond that.

There is no great variation in the appearance of the

hoopskirts, although some are a little larger than others or have more flaring trumpets. The range in color is from snow white to a deep golden yellow. The value of collecting a number of forms is in stretching the unbelievably long season of bloom.

The white hoopskirts come first. They are thought to be too tender for the open garden even in the warm parts of England, but I have forms that flourish, and Billy Hunt says that they have bloomed for many winters in Chapel Hill. Mr. Heath even grows them out of doors in tidewater Virginia, and sometimes has bloom in December. "The weather these little fellows can withstand," he says, "is truly amazing." The tenderest is *N. b. monophyllus* itself, which was called *N. cantabricus* by Clusius. But Mr. Bowles finds it hard to believe that it was ever found as far north as Cantabria, and it is now found only in "the south of Spain, the Balearic Isles, and North Africa." In the sixteenth century it was known as the Cambridge daffodil, having been grown at King's College by Master Nicolas Belton, "a man learned, and a diligent searcher of nature." Master Belton claimed that the palsy could be cured if the patient were seated before the fire and rubbed with the distilled water of the daffodil flowers. Parkinson says that the French called the white hoopskirt *Trompette marin,* a charming name but a little out of proportion if you expect to hear old Triton blow his wreathed horn.

N. b. monophyllus bloomed outside in Raleigh for two years in January or February, unharmed by some of our worst winter weather. Later the bulbs disappeared, but that may have been due more to the situation than the climate, for I had them in full sun, and I have since read that they grow in the shade of small bushes. However, I have also read that the bulbs need a thorough ripening. Whatever the difficulty, this frail flower of frost with its one little leaf is worth any amount of trouble.

The other white forms have several or many leaves. They are grouped under the absurd appellation, *N. b. monophyllus forma foliosus.* (I am still trying to follow Mr. Jefferson-Brown.) These are hardier and much easier to grow than the variety itself. My first little bulb came from Mr. Moncure and lived in my Raleigh garden for ten years. As far as I know it bloomed but twice, once late in November and once in December, although the flowers might easily have been overlooked among the fallen leaves. "How did you find it?" my sister asked when I brought in the first blossom. "Do you go about the garden with a microscope?" The tiny flower is not pure white, but colorless and translucent like a fleck of sea foam. The tube is greenish at the base, and a faint greenish sheen travels up to the tips of the narrow, pointed segments, showing through on the other side and looking like a green shadow. The penetrating fragrance is not perceptible in the winter air, but is brought out by the warmth indoors.

Later, two bulbs, different from each other in the form of the flowers, the blooming period, and from Mr.

Moncure's bulb, came to my Charlotte garden from Mr. Heath, who writes that they bloom with him during any mild spell between January and March. One of these has now been here for five years and has bloomed at various times between the twenty-eighth of December and the twentieth of January. Last year, when I dug the clump, I found that the single bulb had become four, and all of them bloomed this spring after replanting. Their trumpets are flaring, but those of the other little white one are drawn in slightly at the margin. So far the latter has bloomed from two weeks to a month earlier, but this is the only important difference between them. Both have a quaint habit of producing their flowers in pairs. They stand very stiff and straight on their slender five-inch stems. They last two weeks in the garden, even in bitter weather, and show up very prettily against the dark green needles and violet flowers of the winter heath.

The first of the yellow-flowered hoopskirts is *N. b. romieuxi*, which is said to bloom in November but so far has bloomed with Mr. Heath in December, with me in February, and with Mr. Brumbach in late March. Mr. Epstein thinks it should not be planted out of doors in New York, although it comes from high elevations in the Atlas Mountains, and Mr. Jefferson-Brown calls it a hardy bulb. It is one of the most distinguished of the tribe, with its flaring trumpet (an inch and a half across) of a pale and wonderfully luminous yellow. Nylon, a cross between this and *N. b. monophyllus*, blooms in

January or the first days of February. Mr. Heath says that it often blooms in November when well established. I have had as many as four of the milk-white flowers from a single bulb. Their thin, fluted bowls are filled with a strange heady perfume like that of the Chinese sacred lily. Mr. Epstein says it is "particularly free in producing seed, and the bulbs begin to bloom three years after the seeds are planted." [4]

The variety *citrinus*, another pale and large-flowered form, comes into bloom early in March, following *romieuxi*. It is recommended for a cool, moist position in light shade, but the site must be well drained; it did not prosper with me until I planted it on top of a dry wall in full sun.

Next comes the variety *obesus*, which sometimes blooms on St. Patrick's Day. The flowers are the color of ripe lemons, with a refreshing lemon fragrance. They are not at all obese—although perhaps a little portly with their billowing crowns. The leaves are few and thin and serve to show the flowers off to great advantage. Mr. Ingwersen tells of finding the variety *tenuifolius* "in small screes of weathered-down granite detritus at the foot of the walls of the Castelo de Moro near Cintra in Portugal." [5] It is, he says, usually the last to bloom in his garden in England. Last spring it ended the hoopskirt season in mine by blooming in April, but

[4] *Bulletin of The American Rock Garden Society.* January, 1955, p. 15.

[5] *The Daffodil and Tulip Yearbook*, 1951-2, Royal Horticultural Society, London, p. 14.

this year neither the pale, narrow trumpets nor the thin leaves appeared. I think this is another that needs to go on top of the wall.

The late-flowering, deep yellow hoopskirt found in southern gardens is probably *N. b. conspicuus*. My bulbs came from Mrs. Bullitt's garden in Chapel Hill. She had them from Mrs. Le Conte, who brought them to Columbia, South Carolina, from one of the nearby family places that also harbor Queen Anne's daffodil. It is a robust form that increases with great rapidity and is said to reseed, although I have never known it to do so—but perhaps I am too thorough about picking off the dead flowers. The golden flowers bloom in abundance at the end of March or early in April. The stems are shorter than the stiff foliage, which is a disadvantage unless the bulbs are divided from time to time, for there is a great deal of it. Mr. Alec Gray's hybrid, Elfhorn, which blooms at the same time, is the same flower on a smaller scale. The leaves, although they are almost a foot long, are very fine and lax, and do not hide the flowers.

5

Hardy Cyclamen

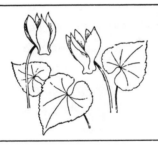

I can well believe the story that an Englishman bought a house in Cornwall because there were so many long-established cyclamen in the garden, for it takes a medium-length lifetime for the corms or tubers to grow large enough to reach their full flowering. Only those who are fortunate enough to acquire them in the size of pancakes can look forward to immediate and lavish bloom. Gardeners who begin with tubers the size of quarters will have to possess their souls in patience, and then in forty years they can expect more than five hundred blooms—perfect miniatures of the florists' cyclamen—from a single plant. The frail elegance of these tiny flowers makes waiting worth while, and in addition the hardy cyclamen bloom when bloom is most welcome; summer and fall and late winter; and where bloom is most needed, in shady places beneath trees.

Their culture is simple. They must have perfect drainage with enough humus in the soil to keep it from drying out, and lime in some form. Mrs. De Bevoise recommends stone chips both in the soil and as a top-dressing. Shallow planting is necessary: barely cover the tubers with soil, or even leave them partly exposed. Do not be discouraged if they do not bloom right away. Sometimes they lie dormant for a year without putting up even a leaf, but then when they do bloom they do it so suddenly that the flowers come as a delightful surprise. Once planted, they should be left undisturbed, for they improve with age and outlive the planter. A yearly mulch of leafmold mixed with wood ashes and bonemeal is the only attention needed. Since they resent being moved, allowance for growth must be made when the tubers are planted. They can be set ten inches apart. Mr. Bowles said that a tuber planted by his mother at Myddleton House in 1856 was still vigorous at the end of a century.

Reports vary on the hardiness of the hardy cyclamen. Dr. Worth considers *Cyclamen neapolitanum* the only one hardy and long-lived in the North, but Mrs. De Bevoise insists that "many species and varieties have proven entirely hardy throughout New England." I should expect most of them to survive the winter in the South, but it may be that certain alpines will find some of our summers either too hot and muggy or too hot and dry. *C. neapolitanum,* at least, adapts itself to a variety of conditions. It flourishes in New England, in Ohio, and on the West Coast as well as in North Carolina. I wish I had known years ago, when I began a collection, that this is the beginner's hardy cyclamen. When I did get to it, it settled down under the oaks in Raleigh and has been equally satisfactory under the pines in Charlotte, both places in the poorest, driest soil.

Neapolitanum is a fall-flowering species, but I have had bloom as early as the Fourth of July. Last year the first flower came at the end of August, and buds continued to appear until early December, in spite of a series of hard frosts that put an end to all other flowers except Chinese violets. The first flowers come before the leaves, resting as lightly as butterflies on their short, stiff stems and looking as if they had settled but for a moment between flights. The color ranges from rose-red to white. The common form is very pale with the faintest shimmer of lilac, and at the mouth are even marks of magenta rose, two to a petal.

When the leaves appear, soon after the first of October, they are as beautiful and as varied as the flowers.

Only Mr. Bowles can do them justice: [1] "It is difficult to find two plants on which the leaves are identical
in shape and also in the pattern of their wonderful
silvery markings. In outline they are circular or triangular, rounded or heart-shaped, with either plain or
toothed margins, and many have pointed lobes like
those of ivy. Other types are long and narrow, like
lances or arrowheads. I have some plants with leaves
glossy and dark green all over, others with wide silvery
margins around very dark green central blotches, and a
few almost suffused with gray and silver."

The foliage remains all winter and into the spring,
but I have never learned how long it lasts because its
disappearance is unnoticed in the excitement of spring
bloom. When the leaves die down it is important to
cover the bare ground with a mulch to nourish the
tubers, whose roots grow from the top instead of the
bottom. And it is well to remember this idiosyncrasy
when they are planted, too, for they will not bloom if
the roots are turned toward the earth.

The old English name for *C. europaeum* is sowbread,
because in the woods of southern Europe the wild
pigs fed upon the tubers, but in Italy they call it *Patate
della Madonna,* and in Switzerland—where the children
stand along the roadside offering them for sale in tight
little bunches—the flowers are known as Alpine violets.
But they are more brilliant and more delicately scented

---

[1] *Journal of the Royal Horticultural Society,* Vol. LXXIV, Part 8,
pp. 325-32. August 1949.

than violets. The color is rose-red. There is something of lemon in their fragrance, and something of honey, and of musk. *C. europaeum* blooms at a welcome time of the year, soon after the middle of June and usually a few weeks before the Neapolitan cyclamen. The stems are only a few inches tall, but the blossoms stand well above the new leaves, which come up in the spring as the old ones die away. Mr. Bowles thinks the plants will prosper only when the foliage is evergreen as in the woods around Lake Como and suggests protecting them from winter wind. Otherwise this species is nearly as hardy as *C. neapolitanum* and so far has proved itself just as readily adaptable to my garden.

C. coum was my first love among the hardy cyclamen. I chose it because it was said to bloom early in the year, and it did not disappoint me in that respect. A small round tuber set out late in the fall produced flowers on the second day of February. Mrs. Lipscomb wrote me that it bloomed in her woods in Greensboro from January until March, the first flowers blooming in the snow. The tiny, sweet flowers vary from red-violet to purple, and there is a white form. Mine were almost a true purple—vivid little things with a dark spot at the base of each segment. The foliage comes with the flowers and is never marbled, but the leaves are dark red beneath.

Although *C. coum* has been in cultivation for more than three hundred years, the extent of its hardiness still seems to be in doubt. It has been known to survive zero weather, and Mrs. De Bevoise included it with the seven species successful at Cronamere, but other northern gardeners have found it unreliable. When I questioned Mr. Starker as to its permanence in Oregon, he answered that the plants lived for years, and added, "I have an old tuber that I'll bet weighs two pounds."

With me *C. coum* has never become established, although I have made several attempts both here and in Raleigh. I think this is because only imported tubers are available, and they come so late in the fall. They should be set out in July. I mean to keep trying until I can persuade it to settle down and live happily ever afterward.

I have been searching for nearly twenty years for the various hardy cyclamen species, with limited success. The difficulty is not only that few are offered, but that those that are available are sometimes misnamed. I have had *C. ibericum* (which the British call *C. vernum*) from two different sources under two separate names, and both of them wrong. Both times I was startled to find the flowers in midwinter accompanied by their leaves, when I had expected them in autumn without their leaves. The flowers of the true species are very like those of *C. coum* and are also scentless. Mr. Bowles finds them even more ornamental. "In the darkest days of winter," he says, "it is cheering to look among the young leaves to find tiny crimson flower buds lying flat on the ground to assure us that before long a mild spell will cause them to rise above the leaves and make a patch of rosy flowers."

In the form I have, the flowers are mallow purple with a wine-dark spot at the base of each of the round, curled petals. They are so brilliant that they quickly catch the eye of the January visitor. Even one tiny flower on a four-inch stem is spectacular. There are paler forms, varying from white to pearly pink. The kidney-shaped leaves, which begin to come up in August, are dark green with a finely engraved silver wreath and wine color on the reverse. The roots of this species and of *C. coum* grow from the middle of the underside of the tubers. Both come from Asia Minor and prefer light shade in a well-drained spot. *C. ibericum* is happily established in my garden on top of a dry wall where it is lightly shaded by the high branches of a very thin pine tree. It does not seem to mind being watered in summer when its neighbors get too dry.

C. atkinsi, a cross between *C. coum* and *C. ibericum,* proved hardy at Cronamere along with both of its parents but has not been a success in North Carolina. Since it is frequently offered, I shall try again. The flowers come (if at all) in early spring and vary in color from white to rose, lilac, red, or purple. They can sometimes be had in separate colors.

C. cilicicum is another that prospered at Cronamere, although not with me. It is demanding as to situation, so I am still searching for the right spot—high and dry and with some shade, as the species grows in the pine

forests of southern Asia Minor. In October Mr. Starker
sent me a tuber with flowers, buds, and leaves. It went
right on blooming after I planted it in the garden, but
tubers planted when dormant have never bloomed before midwinter. The flower is a dear little thing, with a
wine-colored spot at the base of each rosy petal and has
a fragrance that Mr. Bowles describes as like sweet
alyssum and a good heather honey. The leaves are small
and rather round, with a pattern of light green on dark
green above and a stain of rich purple beneath.

Mr. Bowles calls *C. repandum* "a plant that is not
happy anywhere," but adds that "there are certain gardens where it does well and seeds itself freely." My
garden has not proved to be one of those, but Mr. Krippendorf wrote me on the fourteenth of April that he
had found a plant with "six luminous ruby blooms
growing between the roots of a beech tree, where it has
grown without the slightest attention for more than ten
years—maybe much longer." It is a valuable species to
have, for it ends the cyclamen season. In English gardens it lingers until June, when *C. europaeum* comes
into bloom. Thus each season is represented.

I was amazed to find *C. indicum* (sometimes called
C. persicum) on Mrs. De Bevoise's list of hardy species.
She described it as producing white flowers in the fall,
so I suspect that she really had the white form of *C.
neapolitanum*. *C. indicum* is the wild form from which
the florists' cyclamen originated and a tender one, but I
shall try it in Charlotte anyway, if I ever come across it.

C. africanum is also in the references as the florists' cyclamen.

Virginia Stewart [2] gives an account of the hardy cyclamen in her garden in San Anselmo, near San Francisco. "Our staunchest and most successful," she says, "is *C. neapolitanum* which we have grown mostly from seed. Freshness of seed is of great importance in the germination of all varieties of cyclamen. When the single leaf has reached the size of a five-cent piece, we pot them in three-inch pots and grow them on for a year. After that they are ready for larger pots or for setting out in the garden. Pot culture is recommended for gardens that are too hot or where a yearly 'going over' may disturb the corms."

The Neapolitan cyclamen blooms in San Anselmo in September. *C. europaeum* blooms at the same time and keep its leaves for the greater part of the year. *C. coum* blooms in early spring and is hardy in spite of heavy frosts. *C. cilicicum* blooms in the fall and *C. ibericum* in late winter, followed by *C. repandum* in earliest spring. *C. atkinsi* and *C. balearicum* are not entirely hardy. The latter produces small, pure-white, fragrant, and very beautiful flowers in spring, and long gray-green, marbled leaves in the fall.

[2] *Bulletin of the American Rock Garden Society*. Vol. 8, No. 1, p. 5.

6

Colchicums and Crocuses

Colchicum

"I cut the first *Colchicum bournmuelleri* on August ninth," Mr. Krippendorf wrote in October. "We still have *C. autumnale plenum*, and will until hard frost. This year the season will extend at least ten weeks." In my garden early November sees the end of colchicums, but it seems to me that in North Carolina, as in the milder parts of England, we should be able to have them all winter, ending the season in the spring with *C. luteum*. In *Winter Blossoms from the Outdoor Garden*, Mr.

Colchicums and Crocuses

Darnell lists nine that flower between October and February. The only one of these that I have been able to acquire is *C. byzantinum* var. *cilicicum,* which flowers here along with the earliest sorts.

Each season as I come upon names new to me on the importers' lists, I add a few colchicums to my collection, but I never had them in quantity until Mr. Krippendorf sent me a lavish present from his woods. "Wait until you have clumps almost a foot across with from twenty-five to thirty-five open flowers, and buds still coming through," he wrote, and later added that he had counted seventy-seven flowers on a single clump. "The flowers are coming up by the thousands. They light up the woods when the sun is on them. It almost seems that the light comes from within. For colonizing in woodland they are good, and seem to live indefinitely, and in woodland their coarse spring foliage is no detriment."

I have never found the coarse foliage a detriment, even in a small garden, although one is so often warned against it. In the rock garden it takes a little ingenuity to place the bulbs where the stemless flowers will be conspicuous in the fall and where the wide leaves will not be too prominent in the spring. Our warm winters bring the leaves up very early, their tips appearing in January. If the bulbs have been planted well in the background, this new green will be pleasant when the ground is bare, and by the time the foliage has become unsightly the nearby plants will have grown tall enough to cover it.

In North Carolina, another consideration in planting colchicums is to see that they are in a part of the garden where the violet tones of the flowers will not clash with the bright reds of the oxblood lily and the spider lily which bloom at the same time. They should be where they will be seen with the hermosa pink of the hardy begonia and the argyle purple of *Allium stellatum.* They are charming with the purple-spotted toad lilies or the phlox-pink flowers of *Clinopodium georgianum.*

The books recommend a warm, sunny position for colchicums. This may be right for other climates, but I never had any success with them in my garden until I planted them in leafmold in the shade. They need a deep, moist soil, and will not persist in any other, for the bulbs should not dry out entirely in summer. In poor soil, bonemeal can be mixed with the leafmold. A topdressing of manure, put on in the fall after the flowers have faded, is sometimes recommended. Mr. Krippendorf uses no fertilizer. "All I ever do to them is to stick them in the ground and tramp on it," he says, "but of course mine are in virgin woodland. Almost all my bulbs are in shade, and they do all right as to growth even when the limbs of the trees sweep over them. They bloom where not even a fern would grow, but in these places the flowers fall down as soon as the buds open."

For the best results the bulbs should be planted in July or August. Those grown in this country may be procured at the proper time, but the imported ones sel-

dom arrive before the middle of September, when the
flowers are often already emerging from their sheaths.
The bulbs of most species are large, "as large as a man's
fist," Mrs. Loudon says. From their size one would expect to bury them deep in the ground, and where they
grow naturally they are found very deep, but in gardens
they should be planted so that the soil barely covers
them. Once planted they can be left to increase. When
they must be divided this should be done in the summer after the leaves have died away.

From the tuliplike bulbs and the tuliplike flowers it
is easy to see that the colchicum belongs to the lily
family. I do not know why it is called the autumn crocus.
Meadow saffron is the name that the old writers gave
it, but this, along with other pretty old-fashioned names
for garden flowers, has fallen into disuse. In rather general use now is the Latin name which is derived from
Colchis, a country in Asia Minor where the genus is
plentiful. Parkinson, in his *Paradisus Terrestris* (1629),
called the flowers "Naked Boys" because they are "of a
rather naked appearance from want of leaves," and "the
Sonne before the Father," because, by the calendar, the
seeds come before the flowers. "Have you ever noticed
the sequence of the growth of the colchicum?" Mr.
Krippendorf asked; "March: leaves; May: seed; August:
flowers; September: roots."

C. bornmuelleri and *C. autumnale* are narrow-leaved
species, the leaves less than two inches across. *C. bornmuelleri,* from Asia Minor, is the most sumptuous of all.

The tall lilylike flowers come out white, and then the tips of the petals turn to deep lilac. "I marvel at the flowers every time I see them, in spite of the fact that I have known them for forty years," Mr. Krippendorf writes. "I measured several with petals four inches long and an inch wide. This species does not clump up, and I have rarely seen more than five or six flowers to a clump, but it certainly has size and style. The flowers of *C. autumnale* are not so exciting, but they have great charm and are just coming in as the others are going out."

In my garden the buds of *C. autumnale* break into starry blossoms at the end of September. The small pale flowers, of the tint called mauvette, have a silver sheen. Parkinson calls the color a "delayed purple." I suppose he means that it deepens as the flowers age. This is the common meadow saffron native to both sides of the Mediterranean and often found wild in England. In Mrs. Loudon's day it was used for the relief of gout and rheumatism, and was "the principal ingredient in the celebrated *eau médicinale* of the French. It has, however, been found poisonous to some constitutions; and as several persons have died from taking it, the use of the medicine has been prohibited in France, although it is still allowed in England."

Within this species there is much variation in the form, color, and time of flowering. The earliest with me is *C. autumnale major,* which blooms around Labor Day. The rosy flowers are larger than those of the type.

It was disappointing to me to find the variety *croci-florum* in bloom at the same time, for it is described as a winter-flowering meadow saffron, and I had looked forward to having it after Christmas. Otherwise the clear, Chinese-violet flowers are delightful. This native of western Asia should not be planted in shade like the others, but set out in the open where there is enough sun to ripen the bulbs. The variety *album,* a lovely ghost, comes to haunt the garden in October, and the double forms—white and purple and rose-colored—flower last of all.

C. speciosum and *C. byzantinum* are broad-foliaged species with leaves four inches across. These are the ones that are out of place in a proper rock garden because of their wide foliage and spectacular tuliplike flowers, but they make pleasing drifts of autumn color when they are planted by themselves under the trees. The typical *C. speciosum,* which I have grown for a long time, is pretty enough until you have seen the modern hybrids, but the variety *atrorubens* proved to be rather dull and uninteresting. The variety *album,* one of the rare beauties of the autumn garden, has an unfortunately weak constitution. I suppose that is why it is so seldom listed. It will bloom the first season, directly after it is planted, but I have been unable to get it established in either my old or present garden.

All of the others of this group seem to grow exceptionally well in this part of the country, often blooming in August at a time when bloom is most needed. The type once bloomed on the tenth—which I believe is the earliest date that I have for any meadow saffron—and another year Autumn Queen bloomed on the twelfth. This handsome checkered flower of Mathew's purple usually blooms soon after the middle of August, and is often the first one. Violet Queen blooms a little later—usually early in September—producing pansy-violet flowers that measure at least six inches across when they are spread out. The Giant, with flowers to eight inches across, is the largest of all. These are colorful and sweet-smelling. In Raleigh I had a smaller sort, called *C. giganteum,* with faintly tessellated, very fragrant flowers, referred to in Weather's *Bulb Book* as "a fine species of the *speciosum* group from the Zigana Dagh, or Gipsy Mountain."

C. byzantinum is related to *C. speciosum,* but native to the Levant. It was brought to England from Constantinople before the middle of the seventeenth century, and a hundred years later Mrs. Loudon was complaining that it was seldom seen in gardens. In these days it is still rare in cultivation, although, as she says, it is hardy and showy. It was the first colchicum to flower for me this season, opening pale buds on the sixteenth of August. The wide-open flowers are four inches across. The narrow white lines that radiate from the center make a distinct star on the lilac background. This species is very fragrant. The flowers of the variety *cilicicum,* a form from the Taurus Mountains, are larger and rosier and crisper than those of the type, and somewhat tessellated.

The tessellated colchicums are charming. All species are apt to have forms with checkered flowers, but in *C. parkinsoni* the checks are very distinct. Perhaps Parkinson was prejudiced in favor of his namesake when he called it "the glory of all kindes," for the dull blooms that I have grown could not be described as "this most beautiful saffron flower" that "riseth up with his flowers in Autumne, as the others before specified doe, although not of so large a size, yet farr more pleasant and delightfull in the thicke, deep blew, or purple coloured beautifull spots therein, which make it excell all others whatsoever." Parkinson also speaks of its flowering "later for the most part then any of the other, even not untill November," while in my garden it comes with the first, in mid-August or soon afterward.

The small flowers of *C. parkinsoni* are not above eight inches tall. The twisted petals are long and narrow, and checkered with a much-grayed ageratum violet. In spite of their grayness, the warmer violet of the filaments lights the blossoms, and their faithful bloom endears them to gardeners of this part of the country. Mr. Krippendorf says that this species is a shy bloomer with him. Perhaps it likes the South, for Parkinson goes on to say: "Our old country being so contrary unto his naturall, that it will scarce shew his flower; yet when it flowereth any thing early, that it may have any comfort of a warm Sunne, it is the glory of all these kindes."

C. variegatum and *C. agrippinum* also belong to the group with tessellated petals, although their perianths are not so distinctly patterned. The first is a variable species from the Levant and Asia Minor, one of the oldest in cultivation, but seldom seen in the catalogues. *C. agrippinum* is a garden form of *C. variegatum.* It is very like the type, but the leaves stand up straighter and the plant is more robust.

The spring-blooming *C. luteum* is the only yellow-flowered species. And a spring-blooming relative in the lily family, *Bulbocodium vernum,* is often listed in references as meadow saffron.

"I seem to have lost *Bulbocodium vernum,*" Mr. Krippendorf wrote one spring. "Not much loss." I am rather inclined to agree with him, and yet "the meadow saffron of the spring" with its Chinese-violet flowers is rather a welcome note of color when February rolls around. Coming from Alpine meadows, I am sure that they bloom better in cooler climates than they do in North Carolina, although I have read that the bulbs should be taken up at least every second year, and divided before they are replanted. I would rather buy a few new ones from time to time, and plant them in a sunny place to bloom as long as they will.

Crocuses

If all species of crocus were available and could be grown in one garden there would be bloom from midsummer to late spring. In my garden the first buds appear at the end of September, and from then until March the species come along in such close succession that one or another is nearly always in bloom. In a climate like mine, where autumn is apt to be a lingering Indian summer and where winter is often interrupted by intervals of warm, sunny weather, crocuses help to make rock gardening an all-season pleasure. When the weather is mild they bloom delightfully even in midwinter, and some sorts are so careless of the cold that even when the first blossoms are cut back by the frost, new buds will come into bloom as soon as the sun comes out again.

Before the war I started to make as complete a collection as possible of the species, in order to find the ones that would do best in this section. Since many of them come from mountain regions it is to be expected that some will not survive where summers are long and hot and winters are snowless. I had not gone very far with the experiment when it became impossible to get imported bulbs, and I had to confine my collection to the species grown in this country. Since foreign bulbs have become available again, I have added some new species. Most of these have done well so far, but it is too soon to tell which ones will continue to flourish. Even so, most of them are so cheap and so easy to grow that it will be well worth the trouble and expense to have them, even if they bloom for only a season or so.

On the whole, crocuses are easy to grow. They flourish in ordinary loam, demanding only that it be light and well drained. In general the corms should be planted three or four inches deep, but the depth will vary as the corms vary greatly in size. Most species are sun lovers, although in my garden I have found that a number do well under trees.

The name crocus comes from the Chaldean word for saffron. Linnaeus considered all species as varieties of *C. sativus,* the saffron crocus. He divided them into two classes, those that flower in the fall and those that flower in the spring. This division is still followed, but modern botanists recognize about a hundred species, all of them native to Europe or Asia.

The fall-flowering species come into bloom between summer's end and Christmas. For the best results these should be planted in July and August, but in this country this is impossible, for they cannot be had so early from the importers. If they are ordered early in the summer, they will arrive in September, and will do very well if they are set out at once. With some species even later planting is satisfactory.

The first to bloom is *C. scharojani,* which is said to come in July and August, producing flowers of a deep orange yellow. I have long coveted this species, but when I wrote to the importers to ask if it could be had, the answer was yes—at four dollars a corm. Since it is found at elevations of seven thousand feet in the Caucasus Mountains, I do not think that at that price it is a good investment for an impecunious gardener in the middle South.

C. vallicola, also Caucasian, and having creamy-white or pale yellow flowers, is said to bloom in August or September. Imported price: five dollars a corm. Since its name signifies that it grows in valleys, it may be that it would do well at low elevations.

In my garden *C. zonatus* is usually the first to blossom, putting in an appearance late in September, and often blooming on into November. It inhabits the mountains of southern Europe and Asia Minor but takes kindly to gardens, blooming profusely, increasing rapidly, and after a few years reseeding itself freely. In Raleigh, after six years, five corms had traveled from one end of the rock garden to the other. The flowers vary from the rosy lilac of the type to a pure white, but all have the golden zone at the throat, making them look as if they were lighted from within. In the form I have, the flowers are very pale, with an iridescent sheen and fine penciling of deep violet. The species is recommended for full sun, but it does well under the high branches of oak trees, or even under pines. I think it would grow almost anywhere.

The flowers of *C. speciosus* seem very tall because of their long perianth tubes. An English gardener boasts of one that measured a foot from the tip of the petals to the ground. Here they are not more than half that height, which is enough for me. The color is described as blue, but is really a tint of pure violet. Although some of the forms are bluer than others, I have never seen one that I would call a pure blue. In its wide range, from southern Europe to the Crimea and northern Persia, it is extremely variable in both its wild and cultivated forms. In my garden the type has become well established. This year it was in perfection, blooming the first two weeks of October, after weeks of rain, and during an interval of clear, cool weather. The buds are gray and slender, and the flowers never open out flat. *C. speciosus* is a dependable, easy species, and said to increase rapidly. With me the increase is steady but slow. The corms are very cheap, so it is just as well to plant enough for immediate effect. They should be set six inches deep in good leafy loam in the shade. This species will grow in the open but it is one that actually prefers shade, and even likes to be near water.

The yellow-throated flowers of the variety *aitchisoni*, larger than those of the *C. speciosus*, are of a pale hyssop violet, delicately veined in an intricate pattern of purple. They bloom early in October. The flowers of this variety are said to be the largest of the fall crocuses, but those of the variety Cassiope seem to me bigger still. This is a selected seedling of Van Tubergen's, which Mr. Krippendorf sent me last fall. I thought at first that I must have the name wrong, but on looking it up I find it is a variant of Cassiopeia. When I planted the corms late in October, they began to bloom almost at once, continuing in the face of black frost right into December. The flowers, again described as blue, are a

pale, almost luminous tint of violet, lit by a pale yellow
throat and scarlet stigmata. The wistaria-violet flowers
of the variety *globosus* are more egg-shaped than round.
They bloom early in October, and last for a long time.
The bright and shining star of this group is the variety
albus, but I have never seen one in bloom.

Along with these two comes the snowy crocus, *C.
niveus,* of uncertain origin but related to the white-
flowered *C. boryi* of the Greek Islands. *C. niveus* is
described as blooming at the end of October or in
November, but here it is among the first. The flowers
are pure white except for the pale yellow throat, deep
chrome anthers, and orange stigmata. The long, pointed
petals are sometimes slashed near the base. This species
has bloomed here for a number of years, but it has increased little. I have planted it in woodsy soil in the
shade.

C. pulchellus, a small floriferous species ranging from
Greece to Asia Minor, blooms early and long. Buds appear continually from the first days of October to well
into November. The species is well named *pulchellus,*
for the flowers are so adorable that it is hard to describe
them without sounding foolish. Pale, translucent petals
of a grayish tint that is on the blue side of violet, with
delicate lines of dark blue, cup the cream-colored anthers and the orange stigmata. The throat is deep yellow.
Because the flowers are almost tubeless, the thick clusters seem to lie on the ground. When the last flowers are

fading the short, narrow leaves begin to come up, but the foliage does not mature until spring.

Although this species was first brought to England in 1670, it is not mentioned by Mrs. Loudon, and does not seem to be common now. I have read that it is not persistent in New Jersey. My planting has not been long enough established to enable me to tell how lasting it will be. So far it gives every evidence of permanence and increase, and I was pleased to see that it bloomed unusually well after a wet summer. The corms should be planted in full sun in a sheltered part of the garden.

The saffron crocus is the crocus of the ancient world. It is called *C. sativus,* the cultivated crocus, because since the days of Theophrastus it has been grown for the saffron which is made from the dried stigmata and used as a drug, as a dye, and in cooking. Soon after the first of October the leaves come up in a tight sheath, and when they are a few inches high the scented flowers appear among them. The petals are Saccardo's violet, marked with manganese violet at the base. The long, spidery stigma is scarlet, and the anthers are golden. After the flowers fade, the leaves grow rapidly to a length of eighteen inches, remaining bright green and all winter; they do not die down until late spring. This habit of the foliage makes the species unfit for the rock garden, so I have planted it on the herb garden wall beneath a choice Irish rosemary that Mr. Krippendorf gave me. It belongs with the herbs anyway.

Colchicums and Crocuses

With me the corms bloom well the first year they are planted, and less well each year thereafter until they disappear altogether. Mrs. Wilder found the species a shy bloomer, and Mrs. Chalfin says that it has proved difficult in Lynchburg. The only reason I continue to plant it is for the sake of possessing "Saffron, sought for in Cilicia soyle." *C. medius* and *C. longiflorus,* two other late-flowering species, are similar and much more satisfactory.

C. medius, from the French and Italian Riviera, needs a sunny but protected spot and light soil. Since I have had it only three years I cannot promise permanence, but so far it has bloomed well in November and December—one year it lasted until Christmas. The lovely mauve flowers have enough substance to withstand frost, but even if they are killed, more buds appear when the cold spell is over. I cannot find out anything about the hardiness of this species, but it has been through several of our worst winters, and I have read that it wintered in southern New Jersey.

C. longiflorus, formerly known as *C. odorus* because of its delightful fragrance, also comes from the south of Europe. It is found in Italy and Sicily. There is a variety *melitensis* from the Island of Malta. This, too, usually blooms in November, but sometimes there are flowers in October. In the middle of December Mr. Krippendorf wrote: "I still have *Crocus longiflorus* and hellebores. There is one hellebore with eighteen bloom stalks." *C. longiflorus* has done well in both Raleigh and in Charlotte, and along with *C. zonatus* and *C. speciosus* is one of the most persistent and reliable species.

C. cancellatus is a native of the region from the Isles of Greece to Asia Minor. The name means "lattice like," a reference to the coarsely reticulated coat of the corm. I planted twelve of them in September, the year before I left Raleigh. They bloomed well in late October but did not put in an appearance the following fall. I have not seen this species listed since then, but I shall make another attempt when I find it. The large flowers vary from white to violet. In the variety *albus*, which I had, they were silver white with a lilac sheen. The leaves follow the flowers and gradually lengthen during the winter. When spring comes, they are a foot long. It seems strange that after making such good foliage they did not persist.

Several species bloom in midwinter. One is *C. asturicus*, of which Mrs. Wilder writes that it is free-flowering and lovely. Since it comes from the Asturian mountains, it may not do so well in the South as in her New York garden. I have had it but once. A dozen corms planted in September bloomed the first year, from early December until well into January, but the next season produced only a few leaves. The variety *atropurpureus*, with dark flowers of pleroma violet, is the only form available. This species needs sun, protection, and a soil in which there is a good deal of humus.

Another species that blooms for me in midwinter is *C. ochroleucus*. The first time I planted it, the buds came up in a very cold December, and all were frozen before they opened. This year I chanced another dozen corms, putting them in a sunny spot on the south side of the house. There they bloomed all through November, and were stopped only by twelve degrees of frost on the last day of the month. Then, in a warm spell in December, they popped up again. If, once acclimated, the small milk-white, orange-throated flowers could bring themselves to bloom at their proper season, which is fall and early winter, I think they might fare very well.

In my garden the year ends with *C. laevigatus,* which begins to bloom in December and lingers through the first weeks of the new year. Once a single corm produced eight or ten flowers between mid-December and late January. The first flowers were a little marred by sleet, but on sunny days they came out with springlike freshness, even when there was a skim of ice on the pool. Kneeling on the frosty ground, I could catch a faint but distinct fragrance. Warmed in the hand, the flowers smell like hothouse violets. The flowers of this species vary from white to pale lilac.

In the variety *fontenayi,* the only form available, the blossoms are small cups of gray violet; the inner segments pale mauve, the outer ones ageratum violet with precise feathering of a darker tone on the outside. They are lighted from within by the golden throat and stigmata. Along with the flowers come the very fine, grassy leaves that mature in the spring. The corms of this lovely species should be planted in full sun, with sandy loam and lime.

This year the first flower of *C. laevigatus fontenayi* came out on Christmas Day, a day warm enough for lunch in the garden. We were still sitting in the sun when Mr. Krippendorf called. He said that he had been sitting in the sun, too, and that he had taken a walk in the woods, where he found a snowdrop and a Christmas rose in bloom, and a crocus showing color.

I particularly want two other late-flowering species, but they have never come my way. One is *C. salzmanni,* which Mrs. Wilder thought too tender for New York, and therefore recommended to gardeners south of Washington. But it must not be so very tender, after all, for Mr. Free wrote me of its blooming in mid-December in his back yard in Brooklyn, New York, and I have read that it persists and increases in New Jersey —if the mice do not get at it. The corms—if they can be had—should be planted in a warm place, in rich, moist soil.

The other elusive late-flowering one is *C. byzantinus,* commonly called *C. iridiflorus.* It is native to south-eastern Europe, and is a very distinct species because the sharply reflexed outer segments give the flower the appearance of a fleur-de-lis. The unusually broad leaves lack the center line of silver that is characteristic of the genus. I do not know why this crocus is so rarely listed, for it is considered easy to grow in moist, cool, woodland soil and has been in gardens since the days of Parkinson.

The spring-flowering crocuses should begin as the fall-flowering ones depart, directly after Christmas. In favorable seasons they do, but there are years when we have continuous cold at this time, and then there may be an interval of several weeks between the autumnal and vernal species.

Although I found *C. sieberi* difficult to establish in my Raleigh garden, it is the most dependable early species. In Charlotte it has bloomed in January for four years, coming a little earlier each season until it reached the first day of the new year. In Raleigh I have found the small mauve flowers the day after Christmas, hugging the ground for protection against the elements. Since they bloom at elevations of seven thousand feet in the Greek mountains, they think nothing of North Carolina winters. Even after sleet storms they return with the sun, looking as delicately fresh and perishable as ever, the silvery tone of the petals lighted by the golden throat and scarlet stigmata. The comparatively wide, dark green leaves come up with the buds.

It seems strange that *C. imperati,* which grows in the hills near Naples, should not prosper with me in North Carolina, for Mrs. Wilder found it hardy and enduring in New York and Elizabeth Rawlinson reported it as a consistent early bloomer in the Shenandoah Valley. It has never bloomed in my garden at all, although a small patch on the Saint Mary's campus produced a few

flowers for several winters. The flowers are fawn colored in bud, and an intense violet when open. This
species is called the imperial crocus, but it is named for
the Italian botanist Imperati, and not for any royalty.

C. moesiacus, which usually blooms late in January,
takes its name from Moesia, an ancient province of
Hungary, where it was probably first collected; its
range, however, is southeastern Europe to Asia Minor.
It is better known as *C. aureus,* a good name for a
flower that is all pure gold—petals, stamens, and stigmata.
When I saw the flowers for the first time and thought
that they glowed as if there were a light inside, I supposed I was the first to notice, but in 1597 Gerard noted
in his *Herbal* that this sort "hath flowers of a most perfect shining color, seeming afar off to be a hot glowing
cole of fire." The color is variable, ranging from primrose and pale apricot-yellow to the golden tone that
Ridgway calls orange. This is a fine species—fragrant,
floriferous, and long in bloom. Last year a dozen bulbs
that had been planted the fall before produced flowers
from the twenty-third of January to the middle of
March. The buds push ahead of the leaves, which make
little growth until the flowers fade. The corms may be
planted in a sunny place or in the shade of deciduous
trees.

Another golden crocus, *C. chrysanthus,* appears in
gardens in many forms, and among these are found
some of the best of the early-flowering sorts. Mr. Bowles
raised a group which he named for birds. Snow Bunting

is the first to bloom. I think if I could have only one spring-flowering crocus it would be this. The first pearly bud often opens in the middle of January, and the flowering continues for about six weeks. The snowy flowers are tightly furled when the weather is dreary, but the sun brings them out, as fresh as ever, even when the temperature drops to freezing at night. The garden effect is pure white, but the center is gold and the stigmata bright orange, and there is very fine dark penciling on the outside of the petals. The fragrance is delightful, strong, and musklike. The flowers of Canary Bird are not canary-colored, but deep yellow with brown outside. I think Oriole would be a better name. Bull Finch, Yellow Hammer, and Golden Pheasant are some of the other "birds." Then there is the variety E. A. Bowles, raised by Van Tubergen and considered the best of all, with flowers of a wonderful, clear yellow. It usually blooms a little later than Snow Bunting.

C. balansae, from Smyrna, sometimes blooms in January. The flowers are small and numerous, yellow within and bronze without. It is pleasant enough but in no way distinguished.

C. ancyrensis, a sun-loving crocus from Angora (Ancyra being the old name for that city), is advertised as the earliest of all, but did not bloom for me until the middle of February. However, that was a late season, my last in Raleigh, and so the date means little. The flowers are charming and numerous. When wide open they look like small gold coins spilled on the bare ground.

These very early species are a delight at the beginning of the year; but:

> *Crocus hastens to the shrine*
> *Of Primrose love at Valentine,*

and it is in February that the real wealth of bloom comes. I believe I agree with Canon Ellacombe that, to a gardener, "February is almost the most interesting month in the year; in no other month are there so many changes." (In a North Carolina garden and *In a Gloucestershire Garden,* February must be much the same):

"Especially this year when the snow that had been on the ground for weeks disappeared over night, and then after an interval of sunshine with a great uprising of plants taking place, everything in the garden was again sheathed in ice. But the ice melted at the end of three days as suddenly as the snow had melted before. A frog detached himself from the mud at the bottom of the garden pool and sunned himself on its rim; warmth returned to the earth and flowers shone again in the sun as if there were no such thing as winter. In the four seasons there is nothing lovelier than the green, gold, amethyst, and violet of aconite, crocus, and bulbocodium spread over the brown mould in intricate filigree, like the myriads of little

flowers that star the grass of mediaeval tapestries. At
no time is the air softer, or the warmth of the sun
more genial, and at no time do the birds sing more
sadly."

The amethyst in my garden is supplied mainly by *C.
tomasinianus* and its progeny. This species is my favorite, and seems to be everyone else's favorite, too. It
thrives in all kinds of soils and in all climates. It was
named by Dean Herbert for his friend Signor Tomasini
of Trieste and is a native of Serbia, Bosnia, and Dalmatia. It is very wayward in its blooming, which may
take place at any time between the middle of January
and the first of March. The frail blossoms are silver gray
in the bud and variations of red-violet in the open
flower: from the palest tint of lilac to the deepest tone
of hyacinth violet, often darker at the tips of the petals
which are so thin in texture as to be almost transparent.
The flickering color is delightful in the pale sunlight of
late winter and early spring, and as soon as the sun
stops shining the petals are furled again into thin silver
spears. It is this that makes them last so well in the
windy, wet, and frosty weather that is sure to waylay
them at some stage of their bloom. This must be the
most prolific of all species, for in Raleigh my few original corms made themselves so at home under the oak
trees that they spread over a large part of the rock
garden, spilling into the path below, and even en-
croaching upon the other side. When in bloom they

were as impressive as a travel poster of an alpine meadow, but later, when the untidy foliage came up among the squills and daffodils, I began to wish that my already unmanageable garden were large enough to devote a section to each few weeks of spring, or, better still, that a magic wand would wave away the decaying leaves after the flowers had faded.

The poetic name of the Tuscany crocus, *C. etruscus*, was given to it by Parlatore who wrote the *Flora Italica*. This species grows only in the marshy region of western Italy called the maremma. The large scentless flowers are lavender within, with a yellow throat; gray outside, with a satin sheen, and a few delicate feathers of dark purple. They are characteristically globe-shaped. There is a variety *Zwanenburg* which is described as giving "an effect of almost pure blue," but with me this, too, proves to be a somewhat grayed red-violet. Both the type and the variety bloom late in January. Neither persisted in Raleigh, but in Charlotte they are still with me after four years. The species is said to prefer a rich, heavy soil and full sun.

The spring crocus, *C. vernus*, blooms as late as June and July in the Pyrenees, the Alps, and the Carpathians, but it blooms in March (or did, at least, in Mrs. Loudon's day) in the meadows near Nottingham and in other parts of England where it grows wild. It is native in Europe as far south as Sicily. With such a wide range this crocus has many forms, and it is these rather than the type that are usually found in the trade. They vary from white to gray, lilac, and purple, and some of the white forms are striped and feathered.

The yellow crocuses are so garish that to me it seems better to plant them a little distance apart, leaving the softer yellow of the aconite to accompany the lavender kinds. *C. susianus,* a robust and free-seeding species, is planted by itself where the path takes a turn, and where in February the deep yellow stars light the whole section when the flowers are open. When they are closed, the brown-striped buds make a strong pattern of their own. I used to wonder who this Susanna was, that *C. susiana* and *Iris susiana* and other flowers seem to be named for. I thought she must be a lady with a botanist for a lover, or perhaps the virtuous wife of Joachim. But I found that Susiana is an old name for a province of Persia. This crocus, however, has no connection with Persia that I know of. It is a native of the Caucasus, and was sent to England from Constantinople by the sixteenth-century botanist Charles de l'Écluse. In the old days it was called the Turkey crocus, but now it is better known as the Cloth of Gold. Although it is not the earliest, this is the best yellow species that I have had for bloom, increase, and permanence. It is one that seems to do well in all gardens in all climates, for you hear nothing but good of it. Elizabeth Rawlinson wrote in *Garden Gossip* (March, 1938): "A colony of Cloth of Gold crocuses in my garden, planted by my mother forty years ago, sends up punctually every spring green points pushing through the frozen earth shortly followed by orange blossoms feathered with brown on the outside."

Elizabeth was equally enthusiastic about another yellow-flowered species, the celandine crocus: "It settles itself contentedly in our gardens, where its flowers withstand wintry weather very well, doubtless being used to fierce winds in its native habitat." Its native habitat is western Turkestan, Bokhara, and Afghanistan, where it grows in the mountains at elevations up to seven thousand feet. The species is named *C. korolkowi* for General Korolkow, who discovered it in 1882. In Raleigh it did not persist, whether because the sun was too fierce in summer, or the wind not fierce enough in winter, or my garden simply not to its liking. In Charlotte it blooms cheerfully under the pine trees in January—sometimes at the first of the month. In the New York Botanical Garden, it occasionally comes in the middle of January, although it may not appear until the end of February. The flowers are small, delicate, and very fragrant, cadmium yellow within, bronzed without, and burning with a metallic luster.

Another crocus that did not endure in Raleigh is the pretty orange-flowered *C. stellaris,* the Starry Cloth of Gold. Here it blooms faithfully, although late—about the middle of February. Thought to be a hybrid between *C. moesiacus* and *C. susianus,* it is common in the mountains of the eastern end of the Mediterranean.

C. fleischeri, which grows in the mountain meadows of Cilicia, is said to be preferred to all others by the bees, but I notice that the bees arrive with the first crocus of spring, for above each little patch there is the humming sound of summer. The flowers are small but numerous and look as if a breath would chill them, but they stand up sturdily to the frosts of early February. The fine scarlet stigmata, the pale yellow throat, and some inconspicuous dark wine markings on the outside do not detract from the fragile whiteness of the narrow, pointed petals. Pale, threadlike leaves come up with the buds but make little progress until after the flowers fade. The netted corms are tiny, round, and golden. They should be planted in a sunny place in a soil with some lime in it.

I often wonder why *C. biflorus,* a native of Europe from Italy to the Caucasus, is called the Scotch crocus, unless, as Mrs. Loudon suggested, "it be from its extreme hardiness, as the Scotch have a reputation of being an extremely hardy race." It is also called Cloth of Silver, but this name was given by Parkinson to *C. versicolor.* The Scotch crocus is one of the oldest and best known of the species; it was introduced into England before 1629. There are many forms, but the type is white, the outer petals buff on the reverse with three distinct lines of dark purple. The flowers are fragrant. This species blooms about the middle of February, and can be planted under trees. It likes a light soil, and is all the better for some lime.

Mrs. Loudon said that the leaves and even the corms are eaten by rabbits, but my trouble was more with

Mr. Cayce (our springer), who preferred to walk on the ledge where the bulbs are planted rather than on the cinders of the driveway below. The rabbits do eat the foliage of other crocuses, and they are especially ravenous when there is ice on the ground. Cicely says that a generous sprinkling of red pepper around the plants will put an end to these feasts, but I have not the heart to use it when I think of hungry little animals creeping over the frozen earth in search of a green blade, or when I see Molly Cottontail hopping out of a pyracantha thicket and loping diagonally across the garden in order to give Mr. Cayce as long a chase as possible before squeezing out at the far corner.

There are several more spring crocuses that I want to add to my collection, now that I can get them. One is the Corsican, *C. minimus*, described as a little gem for the rock garden, and said to be one of the latest ones, blooming in March or April. I would like to have the small, round, dark purple flowers to round out the season.

7

Wood Sorrels

Oxalis

The wood sorrels comprise a large and widely distributed genus of the family Oxalidaceae with bulbous and
tuberous species, native mostly to South Africa and
tropical and subtropical America. Some of these are
elusive alpines cultivated with great difficulty, some
are well-nigh ineradicable pests, and some are a delight
in a southern garden. For a long time I knew them
only as plants grown indoors in wire baskets and hung

on the porch in summer, and called ox-alice. Now I know that many will prosper outdoors, some even as far north as New York and Connecticut, and that the name is ox'alis.

One of the commonest garden flowers hereabouts, and one of the most valuable, is an oxalis that I had been unable to identify with certainty until Mr. Houdyshel cast some light on it. He sent me what seems to be the same thing, identified as *O. crassipes*. Now *O. crassipes* does not appear in any garden literature that I have at hand, and so I know nothing of its origin or history. But I do know its value. It has pale green cloverlike leaves and tuberous roots. It has a habit of coming up at odd and unexpected places, and is certainly too great a spreader for a choice spot, but I have never had any trouble getting rid of it where it is not wanted, nor in getting it to grow where it is wanted, even in the poorest and driest reaches of the garden. It has flowers of light rosolane purple, with a dark throat made up of fine lines of red-violet. The flowers are in umbels of eight or ten on scapes about ten inches tall, which stand well above the pale mounds of foliage. Here it seldom blooms earlier than April (although once in the middle of March), but continues at intervals during the summer, and in the fall begins again and goes on until frost. If there is no frost, it blooms into November, or even December. There is a pure-white form, too, and it is not such a spreader.

There is an entry in my mother's garden book in

which she notes, on December seventeenth, that the pink oxalis is in bloom along with alyssum, verbena, moss pinks, and the paper-white narcissus, and that we had lunch in the garden against her better judgment. Mr. Houdyshel says that *O. crassipes* is evergreen in southern California and almost ever-blooming, but here it dies down completely in severe weather.

The Mexican wood sorrels are the easiest to grow, but some, and perhaps all, will have to be watched if they are put in the rock garden. If this is understood, they are most desirable for the South. Poking about in Elsie Hassan's shrubbery in the early summer, I came upon the large, decorative leaves of *O. latifolia,* each with three wedge-shaped leaflets peppered with a fine mist of dark red. I begged a clump to bring home with me, and I put it in a choice spot on the rock wall. There I thought the distinctive foliage would show to advantage, and the phlox-purple flowers would be pleasing with the nearby red-violet bells of the Irish heath.

A few weeks later, on a visit to south Georgia, I found George Cobb frantically digging these very bulbs out of his prize dahlias. His chore was aggravated by the rocky soil. But even without the complication of rocks, he said, it is almost impossible to get rid of the deep-seated bulbs once they take hold. I hurried home and carefully removed every one of them from the wall, but I had not the heart to discard the bulbs. I planted them in a part of the garden where they could do no harm, and they went on blooming until the end of October. But the next year no leaves appeared until July, and then only two, and there was no bloom. Whether this will prove to be a pest only in the far South, or whether it is like ivy—"the first year it sleeps, the second year it creeps, the third year it leaps"—and is only biding its time to dig in deeply and forever, I shall not know until later.

Last spring I came upon a new name among the season's offerings, *O. vespertilionis.* "Lilac-rose flowers is all the description we have on this," the importers noted sadly. The flowers were lilac-rose, and very familiar. So were the wedge-shaped leaves, for it proved to be *O. latifolia,* for which I had not been able to find a source. No such species as *O. vespertilionis* appeared in any book in my possession, so I begged Mr. Krippendorf to do some research for me, and he sent by return mail, by the "kindness of Gussie Bowles," the following description of the foliage: "Each of the leaflets is divided at the tip of the midrib and prolonged into two long, forked swallow-tails. In their sleeping posture these wings have been thought to resemble bats' wings, hence their English name." Hence their Latin name, too, for it means "of the bat." Mr. Bowles goes on to say that the plant soon becomes one of the most undesirable of weeds in a warm-climate border, but is "so quaint in leaf structure that it is worth a place in some out-of-the-way corner." All of which sounds irresistible, and I shall not rest until I find the true species, "undesirable weed" though it may be.

Wood Sorrels

Two other bulbous species from Mexico—*O. tetraphylla* and *O. lasiandra*—are much handsomer than *O. latifolia*, and so far these have shown no tendency toward invasion. They have not even spread so much as I would like, for all kinds must be in large patches for good effect. Nevertheless, I shall keep an eye on them, for they may yet decide to run rampant. Since they are summer-growing sorts, I planted the bulbs in the spring, putting them in the shade of oak trees where they do very well, although Mr. Houdyshel says that they should be in sun. *O. tetraphylla* bloomed almost at once after it was planted, sending up a pale slender scape sixteen inches tall topped with a spray of ten or twelve large flowers of Eugenia red. When the bulbs are left in the ground, they do not bloom until late May or June. The four leaflets form a square approximately four inches across, with bands of dark purple forming a contrasting square in the center. They are the most decorative of all. This species is considered hardy, but the closely related *O. deppei* is tender. *O. lasiandra* blooms at the same time as *O. tetraphylla*, with a few flowers on equally long scapes. The flowers are of the brilliant red-violet that is called rhodamine purple, made even more brilliant by the contrasting green of the center. The leaves of this depart from the clover pattern. There are from five to ten narrow leaflets spread out like fingers and sprinkled with small red dots. This seems to be a common garden flower in the Deep South for I often see it advertised by farm women in the *Mississippi Market Bulletin,* and that is about the only place I know to get it, unless you can coax a few bulbs from Mr. Houdyshel.

Several South African species can be had from the Dutch bulb growers. *O. bowieana,* named for a Mr. Bowie who sent it to William Herbert in 1863, is a delightful fall-blooming and winter-growing wood sorrel that is hardy at least as far north as New York. I have had it for several years in the shady rock garden, where it blooms soon after the middle of September, producing large flowers of Tyrian pink which are charming with the fall crocuses. The pale trefoils appear in August and die down in the spring. This year I thought I would try some bulbs in the sun to see if they would do any better (the original shaded clump has not increased) and to my surprise they bloomed the first of May. Mr. Houdyshel says that they bloom either season.

The Bermuda buttercup, *O. cernua,* is naturalized in Bermuda and Florida. Although this is among the most popular of the wood sorrels, I had a hard time finding it. At last it came my way, and bulbs planted in December bloomed early in May. The flowers are large and of a luminous yellow. The cloverlike leaves are small, neat, smooth, and pale gray-green. It looked very weak, and I am not at all sure that it will last outdoors in this climate. Bulbs of *O. hirta* were sent to me in July by a California nurseryman, and have not yet flowered. This is a trailing species with leafy stems and rose-red flowers. I have an idea that it may prove to be a better plant for window gardens than for rock gardens. *O. variabilis* is said to be hardy, but so far I have not been able to find it in the American trade. It gets its name from the variability of the flower colors, from rose to lavender, white or yellow.

O. brasiliensis is the only one of the South American species that has done well with me so far. This is not surprising, for Brazilian plants are apt to take kindly to this climate—sometimes entirely too kindly. I was rather afraid that such would be the case with this small oxalis when I found it growing so freely in Mr. McNairy's garden in Laurinburg, North Carolina, but so far it has kept to itself in the crevices of the stone steps, where it grows in poor, gravelly soil and blooms more lavishly each season. This species is usually described as a greenhouse subject, but I have heard of it in gardens in widely differing climates. In this country it has been grown in South Carolina, where it is called the Georgetown oxalis, and in the state of Washington, where, Mrs. Frye says, it needs some shelter. Mr. Houdyshel says that in California it persists in the lath house but does not grow well in the field. He thinks the winters there are too cold, but I'm sure it has braved much colder weather in Charlotte, where it has proved one of the most dependable of the little bulbs. I should think it would be worth a trial in Philadelphia or even New York—especially as the bulbs are available and fairly cheap, and since it grew—or grows—in Mr.

Bowles' garden at Myddelton House, which is near London and therefore must see some sharp weather.

In northern gardens the main difficulty with *O. brasiliensis* is that it is a winter grower, and the corms cannot be kept out of the ground until spring. I tried keeping them once, and the spring-planted ones came to nothing. Those planted in the fall produce foliage at once, bright green trefoils as round as pennies, with a purple sheen on the underside. As the weather gets colder the leaves seem fresher and greener, and if an occasional extra-hard frost takes them off, new ones soon replace them. The flowers usually come early in April, and continue for more than two months. They are large for a wood sorrel, and of a most intense color, called cyclamen purple.

Mrs. Frye reports [1] success in Seattle with this, and also with *O. adenophylla* and *O. enneaphylla*, "in the close shade of small shrubs, and under the sweeping branches of taller plants." But Mr. Houdyshel writes that he has never been able to get either of them established in southern California. I have been equally unsuccessful in North Carolina, although I have tried both spring and fall planting, and followed all suggestions as to culture. When these suggestions conflicted, I tried both ways. In Washington, Mrs. Frye says, *O. adenophylla* is as "easy as clover," but I am not surprised that this alpine from the southern Andes fails with me. It comes nicely through the winter, and the tiny gray

[1] *Bulletin of The American Rock Garden Society.* Vol. 2, No. 3.

leaves unfold close to the ground in the spring, but they perish as soon as the weather becomes at all hot, and I have never had any bloom. The flowers are large, solitary, and pink. The leaves are divided into numerous narrow leaflets.

O. enneaphylla, from the Falkland Islands, is similar except that the flowers are white with yellow at the base of the petals. Both species are summer-blooming. They are tuberous-rooted, and the tubers should be planted in the fall in soil that is porous but rich in humus. Perfect drainage is essential, but the soil should not be dry.

O. lobata comes from the more temperate parts of Chile, and blooms for me in the fall. The solitary flowers are yellow with tiny red dots. The tubers should be planted in late spring in warm, sandy soil, in full sun. The tiny, cloverlike leaves die away in hot weather but come back again with the flowers. With me the leaves come up right after the bulbs are planted, but once having died away, no more leaves or buds appear thereafter.

Mr. Houdyshel lists another South American species, *O. regnelli,* which he describes as having large white flowers that are everblooming in California, and large truncate leaves that are reddish on the underside. The leaves are trifoliate and evergreen or nearly so. I had this once, setting the tubers out in late spring in case they proved to be tender, but they never came up. Mr. Houdyshel says the tuberous-rooted wood sorrels are apt to be slow in starting, and advises the gardener to keep them moist and be patient. But before patience and moisture had taken effect, I decided to move the sundial, the side on which they were planted, and the oxalis was never seen again.

8

The Iris Family

Bulbous Irises

Most of the small bulbous irises are considered difficult. They come from regions of very high altitude, where the summers are long and hot and dry, and unless the gardener duplicates these conditions the bulbs are reluctant to bloom. You might think that Louisiana summers would be ideal on all those three points, but evidently there is too much rainfall. Miss Dormon takes up her bulbs as soon as the leaves turn yellow in the spring. She pots them in coarse sand and places them in a little greenhouse where they get full sun but are protected from rain. Every fortnight the bulbs are sprinkled lightly, and in September they are planted out again in a sunny part of the rock garden where there is rich loam with plenty of humus. Another method is to hang the bulbs in a paper bag in a sunny window for a few weeks before replanting.

Many of these bulbs possess considerable winter-hardiness, due to their high-altitude origin. I have read that even *Iris bucharica* has wintered successfully in a protected place in the Harvard Botanic Garden.

When I think how *I. persica* has prospered in southern gardens for generations, and in one of them even continued to bloom through a matted clump of star-of-Bethlehem, and how *I. reticulata* was in my great-grandmother's garden in West Virginia as far back as I can remember, I cannot but think that by persistence we could have more of them. Even if they bloomed only in favorable seasons it would be worth it, for these are some of the loveliest flowers that grow. They perhaps seem even lovelier for being unreliable. My own efforts were interrupted by the move from one garden to another. After years of searching, I had just assembled a collection of rare species when I had to leave them behind without knowing how they fared. Now that I am ready to resume the struggle, many are not to be had.

The bulbous irises I have now are planted on top of a dry wall, with ground covers, such as verbena, which survive without being watered. Another good place is at the foot of a west-facing wall, in a bed raised ten inches or more above the ground level. If the bed is under the eaves, it will be protected from summer rains, and if not, a pane of glass propped up a foot above the ground will keep the bulbs dry while they are dormant. A rich, sandy loam is the best medium for them.

There are two groups of the small bulbous irises, the Junos and the *reticulatas*. The bulbs of the first are usually rather big, clumsy things with large, fleshy roots which must be handled carefully when the bulbs are lifted, for they must not be broken off or damaged. The characteristic that distinguishes the flowers of this group is the shortness of the standards, which are spreading or deflexed and often reduced to mere bristles.

The winged Iris, *I. alata*, blooms in the late fall, from November to the new year, according to reports from Louisiana and Oregon. It is seldom listed, and I have never been able to try it myself. The ruffled flowers are of varying tints of blue-violet marked with gold, and with a fragrance described as "something between that of a hyacinth and elder flowers." They are stemless. The broad leaves are about a foot long. This species grows along the western shores of the Mediterranean.

The perfume of *I. persica*, the Persian iris, is so delicate that the saying is that only an aristocrat can smell it. It was brought to England in 1627 for the garden of Queen Henrietta Maria, who was "passionately fond of flowers," and grew in the garden of another aristocrat,

Thomas Jefferson, two centuries later. Jefferson noted in 1812 that six bulbs of the "dwarf Persian Iris" had been sent to him by Bernard McMahon, author of *The American Gardener's Calendar*. I have often wondered if this lovely iris bloomed for the Queen and the President, and if so, whether they were as delighted as I was when I came upon it—a flower as fragile as glass—in my own garden in the middle of February. It was of the palest gray-blue, with dark, velvety purple and a touch of yellow on the falls.

I do not know how far north the Persian iris will grow but I have read of its blooming in two gardens in the vicinity of New York. Mrs. McKinney tells of finding a "sweet, small flower in sea-green, black violet and gold" on the seventh of April, two years after the bulbs had been brought to her garden in New Jersey from an old planting in Tennessee; and Maylou Wild writes in *Horticulture* (August 15, 1934): "In my garden on the south side of Long Island, *Iris persica* sometimes precedes *I. reticulata*. I have had it in bloom as early as March 27. On one occasion there was a light snowfall after the first blossom had opened, and this delicate little flower sat immediately on top of the snow looking like a true ice maiden. The bloom rises not more than three or three and one-half inches above the ground. The standards are delicate little spears, ice blue in color. The falls are white, frilled on the edge, and each has a purplish-black polka dot on it. It remains in bloom almost two weeks. It loves a very dry and sandy soil; in fact, must be planted, if possible, where even the summer rains do not fall too plentifully upon it. Mine is planted where it has an easterly and southern exposure and the eaves of a building reach out, protecting it from the rain. It may be planted under myrtle or any low ground cover because it vanishes utterly from sight as soon as the warmer spring days come. . . . One can scarcely do without it, for such regal beauty is rarely seen in anything so tiny as this little iris."

I. sind-pers is a cross between *I. persica* and *I. sind-jarensis,* a slate-blue flower from the deserts of Mesopotamia. Miss Dormon says it bloomed beautifully for her, bearing flowers of an indescribably soft blue. It did nothing at all under my careless hand, but Mrs. Wilder reported that she had it briefly in Rockland County.

My last fall in Raleigh I planted *I. orchioides,* a species from western Turkestan and Bokhara, and *I. graeberiana,* a recent introduction of Van Tubergen's. The bulbs were kept out of the ground until the first of December, with the hope of discouraging early growth of foliage, but it came up immediately. However, it was not in the least hurt by the cold, and the fragile flowers were equally hardy. The plants of these Juno irises are like miniature cornstalks, less than a foot tall, with the flowers in the axils of the leaves. I thought the flowers of the orchid iris would be the color of orchids, and certainly did not expect them to be aureolin yellow. They are rather curious—though lovely—for the standards are like small bracts, and they droop instead of standing up.

The falls, on the other hand, stand up primly. They are marked with greenish brown. These flowers last three or four days, but those of the other species are fugitive, though numerous. They are in translucent tints of pure violet.

I planted *I. willmottiana* at the same time, and it was about to bloom when the cold caught the buds. I often wonder how these little irises fared after I left them.

Although I have tried it at various times and in various places, I have never been able to get *I. bucharica* to bloom in my garden. However, I have seen it bloom in North Carolina at the end of March, and Mrs. McKinney says, in *Iris in the Little Garden,* that she has had gratifying success with it in New Jersey. As she says, it is a "small plant of Indian corn with ivory, gold-marked, freshly fragrant blooms. It blooms later than the Persian iris, and is the tallest of the group, sometimes reaching two and a half feet."

On the whole the species of the *reticulata* group are hardier and easier to grow than the Junos. The bulbs of these are neat and small, and the four-cornered leaves are as slim as rushes. The flowers are delicately formed and slender, and because of their own brilliance, or from the illuminating touch of the winter sunlight, they have the sparkle of Venetian glass. Those of *I. reticulata* itself are spectrum violet and of an intensity that makes most other spring flowers look washed out. For this reason it is best to let them glow by themselves, or else to allow only yellow flowers to be nearby.

The Iris Family

This species comes from the Caucasus, where it grows at elevations of ten thousand feet, but it has a very wide range; it will adapt to most climates and most gardens as long as it is given good drainage and plenty of sun. It dislikes shade, but Mr. Krippendorf even plants it in the woods. "I find a few occasionally," he writes, "but Lois Brand has them in clumps in the driest, hottest parts of her rock garden." The bulbs are said to bloom better and earlier if they are lifted and dried out in midsummer, but I never bother with this as they bloom early and well in any case. Usually, I find the first flowers late in February, and Mr. Krippendorf often reports them at the same time. "This morning I found *Iris reticulata* in bloom," he wrote on the twenty-second. "They were the first I had seen, although I am sure they had been out for a few days."

There is a form of *reticulata* called *krelagei,* which is described as claret-colored and earlier, but I found it no different from the type in either respect, and I could see no distinction in the varieties Hercules or J. S. Dijt. Then there is the variety Cantab with pale blue flowers which are apt to be too early and too ethereal for the season. This originated in the garden of Mr. Bowles, who called it his turquoise treasure. All of these have the fragrance of violets.

Two blue, early-flowering species from Asia Minor are sometimes described as forms of *I. reticulata. I. r. histrio,* a rare native of the mountains of Lebanon, does well in gardens but I have never been fortunate enough to acquire it. *I. histrioides* is the earliest with me, blooming in January before the leaves appear. The soft blue, fragile flowers last more than a week even in stormy weather, and this is characteristic of the species. Although it is so easy to grow from imported bulbs, it is apt to fail to bloom after the first year because the bulbs split up into small bulbs which take several years to get to flowering size. Also it requires richer soil than the others.

I. bakeriana is a marvel of subtlety in coloring, design, and fragrance. Standards of a soft blue-violet, like the "sun-colored silks of an eighteenth-century boudoir," contrast unexpectedly with the crisp pattern of the falls, in which a patch of white with fine violet dots and a golden crest ends in a tip of blackish purple. The perfume is so elusive—of violets or apple blossoms or spring itself—that it seems to recall a different fragrance to each person. This little iris from the mountains of Armenia is supposed to flower in January or February. It bloomed for me, for the first time, on Saint Valentine's Day. Mrs. Wilder says that it came through the first winter in her New York garden, but did not persist. Even if it does not bloom again, and even if I cannot replace it—for it is fairly expensive and extremely rare—I shall always consider its flowering one of the high moments of the garden.

I. danfordiae, though sometimes grouped with the Junos, looks exactly like the *reticulatas* except for its color, which is bright yellow with olive or brown spots on the falls. This iris is my despair. I have planted it again and again, and never had a blossom. I can see no reason for this, for it is not considered difficult to bring it to bloom the first season, although it sometimes fails later on. I cannot blame my failure on cold weather, for the *I. danfordiae* iris grows at altitudes of four thousand feet in the Caucasus and is perfectly hardy. Since Mr. Moncure grows it in Virginia, where it blooms in February, and since the bulbs are available and cheap, I shall continue to struggle, for many a plant in my garden was despaired of before I decided to try it once more.

Sometimes an unseasonable season—one that is exceedingly wet or dry, a summer of record heat, or a winter milder than usual—brings about the flowering of a plant that has been existing in the garden for quite a while without finding the right conditions for blooming. This seldom-known pleasure came to me like an unexpected present when I found a frail flower of *I. vartani* a few days before Christmas. Until then the bulb had spent two winters with me without producing a bud. I suppose the intense and prolonged heat of the preceding summer brought about the miracle.

This rare iris comes from the neighborhood of Nazareth where it begins to bloom in October. It is the earliest of the *reticulata* group. In California it blooms in December, and Mr. Graves reports it flowered in the Brooklyn Botanic Garden on the sixth day of a very mild January. *I. vartani* is an extremely variable species, which accounts for the conflicting opinions as to its beauty. According to some writers the flowers are a dirty gray-blue and not at all attractive. Others describe it as sky blue, or lavender. There is also a white variety as delicate and translucent as a pearl, and this is the one I have. Some say that the flowers smell like almond blossoms, some that they have the scent of vanilla, and some that they have no scent at all. They also vary in form, but mostly resemble *I. reticulata* in that respect.

Although Dr. Vartan of the Medical Mission in Palestine sent bulbs to England as early as 1883, it is still a rare iris in cultivation. I searched for it for nearly thirty years before I found it at last on an importer's list. This species is for mild climates only, but it has survived a temperature of twelve above zero in my garden, and bloomed after an unusually severe winter. Under favorable conditions it flowers freely, and the individual flowers last for a week.

There is one iris that belongs in a section to itself. It is *I. sisyrinchium*, the Spanish nut, so called because the corms are eaten by the children of Spain and Portugal, where it is native. I cannot remember hearing of this iris until I came upon it on an importer's list, but I find that it has been in cultivation since the sixteenth century. Tiny corms planted late in September produce gray-blue, lemon-scented flowers from early April to the middle of May. The flowers open only in the afternoon, and they are not spectacular, so perhaps they would be admired only by those who, like me, like to grow (at least once) every iris known.

An iris that I really cannot be without, although it requires replanting continually, is really not an iris at all, although it is called *I. tuberosa,* the velvet-flower-deluce. Another old name is widow iris, and because of something sinister in the somber beauty of the dark marks on the olive-green falls, it is more generally known as the snakes-head iris. At present the correct name is *Hermodactylus tuberosus,* which means Hermes' finger, and refers to the shape of the tubers. However, it is still an iris to me, for the flowers are much like those of *I. reticulata* in shape, and the foliage is similar, too. They bloom at the same time in my garden, late in February or early in March. Although it comes from the Mediterranean seaboard, from southern France to Greece, the snakes-head iris is counted hardy. Violet Walker said that in her garden at Woodberry Forest it was long-lived if left undisturbed, and I find that it lives indefinitely in my garden, but does not bloom after the first year. I might have better results if I took up the bulbs, but since they are cheap, it seems simpler to order a few from Mr. Starker in the fall.

Some Southern Irids

Because the little irids that are best known in this country are gay Cape bulbs usually associated with California or with window gardens, I used to look upon the tender bulbs of the iris family with halfhearted interest. In this I was altogether wrong, as I learned from my dear Mrs. Dormon, who introduced me to some little-known treasures from the lower South, and from Miss Caroline Dormon, who has pictured them so perfectly in her beautiful book, *Wild Flowers of Louisiana.*

The flowers of *Nemastylis acuta* are called celestials, and rightly so, for as Miss Dormon says, "of all the lovely members of the iris family, this is one of the most exquisite, with fragile, lavender-blue flowers that look as if they would melt with a breath." In appearance they have not the typical form of the family, but look like wide, flat, chicory-blue blossoms of a large-flowered clematis. There are three long segments and three shorter ones, all pointed. The yellow anthers stand close together, like a tongue, in the middle of the white eye, their tips curled like fern fronds. Between them the fine, threadlike branches of the stigma merge in pairs. The flowers are almost scentless, but it seems to me that there is about them a pleasant freshness, as of lemonade. They bloom here and in Louisiana in April, although Mrs. Dormon said she had had them in her rock garden in March. She told me to plant the small, dark bulbs in sun or shade in any good soil. However, they disappeared without blooming when I planted them in a damp place that most rain lilies like. Those in the drier soil of the rock garden, where there is leaf-mold but no manure, have bloomed for several seasons. In Texas, celestials grow on the prairies, but Miss Dormon says that in Louisiana she has found them only in "open shortleaf pine woods, in heavy clay soil." They are found from six to twelve inches deep where they grow wild, but it is not necessary to plant them so deep in the garden.

Although *Herbertia drummondiana,* better known as *H. caerulea,* grows on wet prairies along the coast of Louisiana and Texas, it does not hurt the bulbs to be in dry soil in the summer. Note: They must not be lifted. In my garden they bloom in sun and in shade from late April, or more often early in May into June. They make their growth in the winter, and the short, narrow leaves disappear before the seed pods ripen. The flowers are intricately designed in interlaced triangles. There are three oval, petal-like sepals of deep lavender with the white claws of the sepals flecked with purple spots, three small and pointed petals of pleroma violet, and three stamens in the center. There are several scentless and fugitive flowers on the wiry stems. The stems are from five to nine inches high; the leaves grow to about the same height. The herbertias in my garden have persisted, but even though they seed well, they have not increased, for I always collect the seed. Last year I sent some to Mrs. Hassan, who said that by spring she had bulbs of a size suitable for transplanting. Mr. Pearce lists *H. pulchella* as a tender sort, with fragrant blue flowers.

Eustylis purpurea, which grows in dry, sandy, longleaf pine woods in Louisiana, is called the pine-woods lily. It is not at all like a lily, but is triangular like its relative the tigridia. In fact, it is sometimes offered as the blue tigridia. The three large outer segments of the flower are a shimmering aconite violet, and the short inner ones are a velvety prune purple with a distinct white mark and tiny touches of pale yellow. The center is mottled with an iridescent pinkish brown that, in combination with the delicate violet and dark purple tones, is very handsome. The flowers last only a few hours on hot days, but when it is cool and overcast they keep fresh until evening. They are on tall, thin stems, but even though tall they are not out of place among small plants, and the narrow, plaited leaves will not shadow the lesser things. They begin to bloom in late May and continue to bloom through the summer if the ground is moist. Mrs. Dormon said that the bulbs could be planted in sun or shade, and in sand or clay, but that they must not be more than two inches deep. I have read that the pine-woods lily will flower the first year from seed sown in late autumn, and that the bulbs may be left in the ground as far north as Philadelphia, with slight protection.

All three of these little bulbs are best planted in the fall, for they begin to put out roots quite early and need to be established if they are to bloom the first spring.

The Honorable and Reverend George Herbert's cypella, as Mrs. Loudon calls *Cypella herberti,* also came to me from Mrs. Dormon, who said that she liked it better than tigridia. I doubt if many will agree, for flowers of the cypella cannot compare in size and color with tigridias, but in my garden, as in hers, it is much more reliable and much longer in bloom. It has bloomed for four years now, beginning early in May and blooming on, after a midseason rest, into August or September. The flowers are the warm golden color that is called deep chrome. There are three dark purple lines radiating from the center, a sprinkling of fine maroon dots, and a little white trimming. They are intricately fashioned in a design of circle and triangles, the three outer segments indented in the center to form a cup which gives the genus its name. Within the cup the three inner segments form a smaller triangle. Cypella grows in my garden on top of the little wall where the bulbs that like a summer baking are planted. It blooms in dry weather, even though it is never watered, and seems to thrive in the light soil and the full sun. The flowers are on slender, three-foot stalks. This sounds very tall, but they are not at all out of place among the smaller bulbs, and the color is delightful in early summer with the blue violet of *Brodiaea coronaria.* It seems strange that this attractive, easy, and persistent bulb that grew in Mrs. Loudon's garden more than one hundred years ago should still be so little appreciated. It comes from Mexico and South America, but fits in with these little irids of the Gulf Coast.

Cape Bulbs

I have not given up all hope of growing the Cape bulbs. In the Far South some are much planted, while others are at their best only in southern California where the cool nights and hot days are like the climate of South Africa.

IXIAS

The ixias are grown out of doors in California, but Mr. Hayward says that they last for only a season or so in Florida. In Raleigh, where they are hardy and persist for several seasons, they are well worth planting even though they are not permanent. After several failures, I planted a dozen mixed bulbs at the foot of a south-facing wall. I planted them at the end of December so that they would not make early foliage to be cut back by frost. Several bloomed early in April of the first season. There was one about two feet tall with delicate pure-white flowers; one with citron-yellow flowers with a center of Hay's maroon; and one clump of flowers of aster purple with the Indian lake in the center. The next season none of these bloomed again, but one that had not bloomed before opened bright-colored buds in the middle of May. These flowers were the gayest of all. The petals were of that stirring color that the horticultural chart calls Saturn red, with a spot of red-violet in the center, circled with dark red-brown.

The flowers were very large, nearly two inches across. When these die out I mean to plant some more, for they are not expensive. The bulbs are best planted two inches deep in rich, sandy soil in a sunny place. No animal manure should be mixed with the soil.

TRITONIA

Two small tritonias—*T. crocata* and *T. hyalina*—can be grown in the same way as the ixias, to which they are closely related. In fact they were formerly called ixias. They are said to be hardy when once established, but I have not found them as permanent as the tall garden hybrids that bloom in the summer. However, the corms are cheap, which makes yearly renewal practical. They can be planted in November to bloom in May, when the garden is at a low ebb between spring and summer bloom. They flower on short, branched, wiry stems that spring from a tuft of narrow leaves.

T. crocata blooms in mid-May or a little earlier. The petals are saffron or grenadine, scalloped and spotted with yellow or red or brown. There is a series of named varieties in orange and scarlet and salmon, but the only variety I have grown is the old-fashioned one called Prince of Orange, which is not orange at all, but a brilliant grenadine red.

T. hyalina, sometimes called the flame freesia, blooms at the end of May. It is another small flower of bright, delicate tones between red and orange, with gay markings of light on dark or dark on light. Mrs. Loudon described it as a "blaze of brilliancy." The specific name refers to the hyaline membranes at the base of the flower, curious transparencies like little windows, that are characteristic of both species.

HESPERANTHA

So many new things have been creeping into the catalogues recently that every season is filled with the excitement of flowers blooming for the first time. One of the novelties is hesperantha, another bulb of the ixia group, and formerly placed in that genus. Hesperanthas have been in cultivation since the eighteenth century. Mrs. Loudon grew a number, but not *Hesperantha Standfordiae* which is of recent introduction and seems to be the only one offered at present. Six corms planted in November produced eight-inch spikes that bloomed continuously from the fourth of April to the middle of May. Hesperantha (or hesperanthera, according to Mr. Pearce) means "evening flower," most of the species being night-bloomers, but the flowers of this species open at noon and close at sunset. Although they are so fugitive, so many blossoms are crowded onto the slender stems, and the petals are of such a luminous yellow, they make a good showing while they last. This has already become my favorite of the Cape bulbs, and even people who never notice anything smaller than a dahlia were moved to ask its name when they saw it in bloom in the garden.

The Iris Family

Along the eastern seaboard, freesias are too tender for any gardens except those in the most southern parts of the region, and even in Florida they cannot be left in the ground through the year. There they must be dug after blooming and stored until fall because of the summer heat. In Florida they flower in February and March. Mr. Hayward says that they should be planted in sandy garden loam, and that if there is any doubt about the root-knot nematode, the soil should be treated with D-D or other nematicide two or three weeks before planting. Freesias should be planted early, in September if possible, and not later than the end of October.

BABIANA

The color of the flowers of the babianas ranges from blue-violet to red-violet; they are sometimes called blue freesias. I think they are about as hardy as ixias, and should live through the winter in the middle South in a protected sunny situation, but they have never bloomed for me. I thought they would be particularly good for the rock garden, because they are less than twelve inches tall, but they are not for gardens where there is no dry season to give them a period of rest.

SPARAXIS

The sparaxis is called the wand flower. It is related to the freesias and requires the same culture except that it is hardier. It will survive a winter in this part of the country, and may bloom the following spring but is not likely to persist.

STREPTANTHERA

Streptanthera cuprea is the smallest of the dwarf South African irids, growing only six to eight inches tall. It is grown on the West Coast, and is said to be hardier than the freesias, but I have never had it. The flat, six-petaled flowers are the color of a tangerine.

LAPEIROUSIA

According to *Hortus Second, Lapeirousia cruenta* is hardy in the North with winter protection, and so the fault must have been with me when it failed to live through the winter in North Carolina. Violet Walker reported summer bloom in Woodberry Forest from plants raised from seed. In Florida it blooms in the winter. The flowers are carmine with darker spots on the lower petals. The one-sided racemes are from eight to twelve inches tall. The corms should be planted three or four inches deep in well-drained soil. They respond to a mulch of old manure.

Mrs. Loudon says that the genus was named by the French botanist Abbé Pourret in honor of Picot, Baron de la Peyrouse. The Baron, she says, is not to be confused with the "celebrated and unfortunate" Comte de la Peyrouse, the French circumnavigator. *L. cruenta* is apt to be listed as *Anomatheca cruenta*.

The Iris Family

Moraea blooms in gardens in Florida and southern California but the bulbs have never survived with me. However, I am still trying. Mrs. Dormon said that they grew out of doors in Shreveport, Alabama, and Mrs. Hassan wrote from Birmingham that *Moraea polystachya* had bloomed for a long period each fall for four years. In California it blooms in the winter. I once set out the peacock iris, *M. glaucopis,* in March, and it bloomed the same season, but never gathered itself together to flower again. The flowers are lilac with yellow spots. The round, white outer segments are marked at the base with a dark metallic spot like the eye of a peacock's tail. This is a low-growing plant, with stems usually less than a foot tall. These two species, like most moraeas, grow from corms, and require the same treatment as freesias.

In the subgenus *Dietes* the rootstock is a rhizome. The species of this section require the same treatment as standard irises. Mr. Giridlian says that they are hardy wherever the fig grows, and so I gave them more than one trial in North Carolina, but those that came through the winter got off to a slow start and none of them bloomed. In California they bloom all through the summer in sun or shade, in any soil; they endure excessive moisture as well as too little. *M. iridioides* has white flowers with yellow and blue markings, and *M. bicolor* has yellow flowers marked with brown. Both are low-growing species, sometimes listed as *Dietes.*

HOMERIA

In the *Gardener's Chronicle* for February, 1948, Lester Rowntree wrote of two delightful-sounding South African irids for California gardens—homeria and romulea. Eager to see what they would do in North Carolina gardens, I started to search for sources. So far I have found none for romulea, although Mr. Pearce sometimes offers the seed. Mr. Giridlian has listed homerias.

Homeria collina can be planted in the spring for summer bloom in climates where it is not hardy. Mrs. Loudon says that the bulbs should be taken up after blooming to give them a rest period, and that they should be planted out again in February or March to bloom in May. They should be kept in a cool cellar so that they will not start into growth too soon. Mrs. Rowntree describes the flowers as the darkest shade of shrimp red in the horticultural chart, with a pale yellow star edged with Saturn red in the center.

ROMULEA

Romulea rosea, named for one of the legendary founders of Rome, was known to Mrs. Loudon as trichonema, and classed as a greenhouse plant. But in the *Cyclopedia of Horticulture* it is described as suitable for outdoor planting, although less hardy than the crocus which it resembles. Mrs. Rowntree says that the yellow-centered orchid-purple stars appear in January on three-inch stems. They last for only a few hours.

9

The Lily Family

Allium

Traveler pluck a stem of Moly

"Everybody who has read Homer's *Odyssey*," Mrs. Loudon says, "knows that Ulysses could never have descended into the infernal regions if he had not turned the dog Cerberus into gentleness by a sprig of the herb Moly, which he held in his hand. Now the herb Moly is no other than the yellow-flowered garlic, which smells strong enough to frighten away any dog, even without his possessing a triple sense of smelling." It is evident that Mrs. Loudon herself was not among those who read the *Odyssey:* Homer's flower could not have been the yellow-flowered garlic, for it was white, "like to milk." But I am ready to put my faith in *Allium moly* if sheer beauty has any magic against the powers of evil. However, the daffodil-yellow flowers have never seemed quite so golden in my own garden as they did when I first saw them in late May in the New York Botanical Garden's Thompson Memorial Rock Garden. It seems odd that this flower of the Spanish woods should bloom with more abandon in New York than in North Carolina, but so it does. It does not increase with me, either, but Mrs. Loudon said that her only difficulty was to keep it from covering the whole garden "to the exclusion of all other plants." I have always liked lily leek as a common name for *A. moly*. Not that it looks or smells at all like a lily—on the contrary—but because I like those languishing William Morris names.

A. flavum, another yellow allium that is much admired, produces loose umbels of pale primrose flowers in June in my garden, in July in New York. The tiny variety *minor* or *minus* is better than the type, and seeds itself in odd places, although the individual plant is not long-lived. Much better than this, as I know it, is *A. Coryi* of the mountains of southwestern Texas, where, early in April, it blooms on the mesas at altitudes of more than six thousand feet. Trials in San Antonio

proved it a willing bloomer in a dry, hot climate as well
as in the cool, moist air of the mountains. My acquaintance with it is brief, as Miss Kell sent it to me the spring
we left Raleigh. The delicate chrome-yellow flowers,
about seventeen to an umbel, bloomed at the end of
April on short purple scapes. Lieutenant Thad Howard
describes them as being much like *A. Drummondi* in
form, and as varying in color, from buff to gold. "A.
Coryi would be desirable for its color alone," he said,
"but its tidy habits and dainty sprightliness make it a
real acquisition to any collection of rare alliums." [1]

At present I know of no source for *A. Coryi*, but this
year I had from the Oakhurst Gardens in Arcadia, California, three other recently introduced Texas alliums
that Lieutenant Howard writes about in the same issue
of *Plant Life*. One of them is *A. Drummondi*. I think it
would have been the first to bloom if it had come up,
but it never did. This must have been the little un-
named species that Miss Kell sent me several years ago,
a double handful of tiny bulbs that bloomed the first of
April. As they had been planted, I think, just before
they bloomed, and as the Oakhurst bulbs were planted
in the fall, I shall try putting out the next lot in March.
Miss Kell's flowers were wonderfully fragrant—a characteristic of *A. Drummondi*—with the sad, spicy odor
of pinks; the starry flowers were imperial purple. Lieutenant Howard says that this is a widespread species
with flowers shading from white to deep rose-purple,

[1] *Plant Life*. Vol. 10, No. 1, January, 1954, p. 109.

and that it is "capable of making a real color splash when thickly planted. This is particularly true if the planting includes selections of the full color range. The individual flowers are interesting in their variety of patterns and shades, some flowers being solidly colored, while others are pink or white with dark stripes down the center of each petal; still others are red or pink with white centers or 'eyes.' Even the shape of the flower varies." Mrs. Henry grows this out of doors at Gladwyn (Pennsylvania).

The next of these to bloom is *A. mobilense*, whose lilac spheres last throughout the month of May. This is a taller one, to eighteen inches, but the effect is delicate enough to allow of its being called a little bulb.

Since *A. zenobiaea* is more expensive than the others, I had only a single bulb, and just as it was about to bloom I flipped the hose across the terrace and neatly beheaded it. Now I shall have to wait for another spring to see what Mr. Giridlian calls the finest of alliums and the botanists regard as the queen of the Texas wild onions.

All of these Texas species like full sun, good drainage, and a neutral or slightly acid soil. *A. mobilense* requires a steady supply of water in the growing season.

Three small, spring-flowering alliums with white flowers are great favorites of mine. *A. triquetrum*, the three-cornered Moly, is the earliest, blooming from the end of March into May. It is more like a squill than an allium, with its nodding campanulate flowers; there are from three to seven small white bells delicately striped in green and hung on a three-cornered stem. This species likes shade and moisture, although it will flourish anywhere and come up from self-sown seed in all sorts of unexpected places—but always in the right one and at the right time. In all of the years that I have had it, there have never been too many seedlings—in fact, I have never had an allium (except our wild garlic!) that spread too freely, although a number have that reputation.

The Naples onion, *A. neapolitanum,* is a tender bulb. Although Mrs. Wilder sometimes succeeded in wintering it in New York, it is not considered hardy north of Philadelphia, and even in my garden it must be in just the right spot if it is to be at its best. The right spot is at the foot of a low south-facing wall. There it blooms at the end of April (or sometimes earlier) and continues in beauty for four weeks, its immaculate white flowers fresher than the spring.

The third is *A. zebdanense,* named for a village in Lebanon where it grows at an elevation of six thousand feet. This, too, I saw first in the New York Botanical Garden, small clusters of snowy cups floating on tender stems. I searched for it for ten years before I found it on an importer's list. Now I shall have to try again, for the bulbs survive only in a very dry place and with sharp drainage, and the spot I chose was damper and shadier than I thought. In the end I may find that it is not an allium for this climate. It flourishes in Canada, where it blooms in June, and in New York, where it blooms in May. Here it came into bloom on the twenty-first of March.

The West Coast species have not, in general, done well with me. The best is *A. unifolium,* which grows in grassy meadows and along the streams of the Coast Range from northern California to Oregon, and which, according to Lester Rowntree, is the one that grows most readily in gardens if it is treated to heat, moisture, and a rich soil. It bloomed in Raleigh in late April or May. The rather large flowers, of a pleasant gray-violet, are in many-flowered umbels on eight-inch scapes. The western alpines—so far as I know them, which is not very far—have not been good subjects for southern summers, but Bernard Harkness says they did well in his garden in central New York, in a lean, gravelly soil.

One more small allium for spring (that is, it blooms here early in May, but I found it in bloom on the first of June in the New York Botanical Garden) is *A. ostrowskianum* from the Alps of Turkestan. It is a stumpy little thing, four inches tall, with flowers of magnolia purple.

Blue garlic, *A. caeruleum,* blooms in my garden in late April or early May, and about a month later in New York. I have never managed to keep it long, but I buy a few bulbs from time to time, for they are available and cheap, and the spheres of Windsor blue are like no other flower that grows. This perfectly hardy species is very generally grown, and blooms easily enough the first season, but better gardeners than I have found it difficult to establish. It comes from the steppes and deserts of central Asia and requires a dry, hot situation.

There is a group of alliums called the "bluebell garlics" from the mountains of northern India and China. They are small and choice, with fine grassy leaves and dainty flowers that in the best forms are described as a true blue. These usually dry up in my garden before summer has well begun. *A. cyaneum,* the only one that ever bloomed, produced flowers of wistaria violet in the middle of June.

I am now leaving these choice alpines to gardeners who live where the summers are cooler and contenting myself with the duller but more reliable sorts that bloom on and on in muggy weather, their pale lavender flowers and gray-green leaves filling gaps in the front of the borders. *A. Aschersonianum,* a native of Asia Minor, takes to hot weather; it blooms in early summer, with a second round in August. The flowers and leaves resemble chives. *A. subroseum* is similar but smaller, neater, and later. This is described as bright rose-pink with no hint of lavender, so it may be that there are better forms than the one I have. Taller stems, with fluffy heads of a clear opalescent red-violet, make *A. tanguticum* one of the best of the late summer species. As far as I know, it is not in the trade. Mine came from Virginia, where it passed from garden to garden, and

Raymond Freeman writes [2] of its growing in Illinois from seed planted outdoors in early spring.

Brodiaea

Like so many native American flowers, the brodiaeas were found, described, and named by the British. The genus was founded on *Brodiaea coronaria* which was discovered by Mr. Menzies in 1792, or so Mrs. Loudon relates, and brought to England by Douglas in 1826. Sir James Edward Smith named it in honor of the Scotch botanist, James Brodie.

The brodiaeas are mostly natives of our West Coast, where they range from the plains to hillsides and mountaintops. There are conflicting reports as to their performance in the East. Carl Purdy, in his now-more-than-ever invaluable catalogue (and if you are lucky enough to have kept one, cherish it) notes that *B. capitata, B. lactea,* and *B. laxa* are considered "absolutely hardy and long-lived" at the Harvard Botanic Garden, and adds that if these are hardy the rest should be. But eastern gardeners do not always agree with this. Most of them find, as I do, that some species are permanent and some are not, the difficulty being more with wet summers than cold winters.

The corms are planted in the fall, from October to November. Mr. Purdy says to plant them two inches deep in rough, gritty soil, and leave them alone. Drain-

[2] *Plant Life.* Vol. 9, No. 1, January, 1953, p. 64.

age is the important thing. A light soil is recommended, but Mrs. Rowntree says that most species are standbys for heavy clay. I found this to be true in Raleigh, where the clay must have been the world's hardest and poorest. The corms should be planted in quantity for effect. This can be done without taking up too much space, for the scant foliage has often dried up before the flowers bloom, and the slender scapes are very graceful above low-growing rock plants.

Mr. Purdy divides them into two groups: the early-blooming woodland species and the late-blooming harvest brodiaeas.

The woodland brodiaeas grow best in the shade of deciduous trees. *B. capitata,* called blue dicks, is the earliest and commonest. "It is probably one of California's most widely distributed plants," Mr. James writes.[3] "It grows from sea level nearly to the tree line in the mountains, and also in the hot interior valleys. I know of no especial effort to bring it into our gardens, probably because it is so widely distributed. And yet to my knowledge it is one of the easiest plants to grow, and the flowers improve so much in size and number under cultivation that you would hardly recognize it as a common wild flower. The violet-blue blossoms are borne in a close cluster on the end of a slender stem, twelve to eighteen inches high. They cut well and are most attractive. Occasionally the stems are three feet high when growing under shrubs. It has only one or two

[3] *Herbertia.* Vol. 3, 1936, p. 126.

narrow leaves and they lie nearly prostrate. It is propagated easily by seed (forming corms that bloom in
three years) and slowly by cormlets. It does best
planted four to six inches deep in a medium sandy loam,
either in full sun or in partial shade, but will do well in
any soil provided there is good drainage. Those conditions plus a definite rest period are the only things it is
fussy about. It is hardy under all except the lowest temperatures. In Santa Barbara it starts flowering six weeks
after being planted, and continues for three or four
months." I think this pretty well sums up the ways and
needs of most species.

The blue dicks blooms in March in California; in
March (or more often in April) in my garden; and in
May in Mrs. Wilder's. It is the easiest of the brodiaeas
to grow, but I must say that I have never found the
dull lavender flowers at all attractive. And yet, as with
some dull people who never fail to turn up at regular
intervals, you eventually get to be rather fond of them,
especially since the umbels last for a month. Mrs.
Rowntree describes a deep, rich purple form as an im-
provement on the type.

B. douglasi, said to be "super hardy," blooms about
the same time, although it is sometimes caught by a late
frost which pinches the stem and makes the heads
droop. But this does not happen often enough to matter, and the wide umbels of translucent blossoms on
eighteen-inch stems seem very graceful among the
more stolid spring flowers. The light violet petals and

the blue-green anthers have a coolness that is pleasing with the soft yellow of cowslips and the pallor of the rock-garden daffodils.

The many-flowered umbels of *B. bridgesi* begin to bloom between the middle of April and the middle of May. Mr. Purdy says that there may be fifty flowers to an umbel. The flowers are lavender with a deeper sheen and the delicate finish of a seashell. The scapes are shorter than most, not more than twelve inches. *B. laxa* is similar, except that it blooms later—usually early May, but occasionally the end of April—and the flowers are a deeper violet. They are called triplet lilies. A more poetic name is Ithuriel's spear, but they must have burned with a bluer flame in the garden of the person who named them, if they appeared like the sword of that bright angel who put evil in its true light.

The two yellow-flowered species are similar, at least as I have grown them, and both are temporary unless lifted. I am much too lazy to take this trouble, but fortunately they are inexpensive enough to make it worth while to replenish the stock from time to time. *B. ixioides* is called Pretty Face. It blooms in early April, and a single umbel lasts for a month. The wide umbels are on short stems, less than a foot tall. The flowers are Pinard yellow with apple-green stripes on the reverse of the pointed petals. The flowers of *B. crocea*, the golden brodiaea, are a deeper yellow.

I seem, somehow, to have left out *B. lactea*, the wild hyacinth, which is one of the best. Mrs. Wilder says that it is easy, endures and increases in her garden, and blooms in early June. With me it holds its own, and flowers in May. The very fragrant flowers are white or lilac cups with the characteristic bright green midribs on the segments. Unlike the others, it prefers low, moist ground.

The harvest brodiaeas are so called because they grow in the hay fields, and the flowers are cut with the harvest. In California they bloom in June and July, but here they bloom at the end of May, or sometimes a little earlier, and last only until the middle of June. They require full sun, and will not bloom in the shade. *B. coronaria*, usually offered as *B. grandiflora*, has grown and bloomed in one spot in my garden for more than ten years without ever having been given any attention, and Mrs. Wilder mentions it as one that lasts well in eastern gardens. It is partial to heavy clay and moisture, but here it flourishes in hot, dry, sandy loam, blooming equally well in wet seasons and dry. The glowing amethyst flowers are characteristically striped on the reverse with bright green, and the petals shine as if they had been lacquered. There are several in a wide, loose umbel, on twelve-inch scapes. The flowers of this and *B. californica* are very large, an inch and a half or more in length. There are two color forms of the latter, one with flowers of petunia violet and one with bluer flowers. *B. californica* is not long-lasting with me, and neither is the other harvest brodiaea, *B. eastwoodi* or *eastwoodae*, a charming white-flowered species.

I know of only one South American species in cultivation in this country, the spring star-flower, *B. uniflora,*
native to Argentina. This is very prolific and common
in gardens in the South, and is often known as *Triteleia
uniflora.* It is very different from the North American
brodiaeas. The solitary six-pointed stars are milk white,
with a violet wash and dark wine stripes on the reverse.
They are very fragrant, but the stems and leaves smell
of garlic. The gray-green allium-like foliage comes up
in the fall and dies away after the plant has bloomed.
This is an invaluable small bulb for spring, for it blooms
early and long, often from the first of March well into
April. It will grow in any soil, no matter how barren,
in sun or shade, and I am frequently glad to have it to
fill in a bare spot, but I would never plant it among
choice rock plants for it is too much of a spreader. It is
not a pest, however, and I would not want to do without it entirely. The flowers are on short stems, to about
eight inches, standing just above the grassy tufts of the
leaves. This species is hardy at least to Washington, and
I have read that it will endure in Philadelphia and
Ohio.

Milla

Milla and *bessera* are summer bulbs that can be planted
in April for bloom in July and August, and lifted in the
fall for winter storage. Bulbs left in the ground have
never bloomed for me a second season, but Violet

Walker reported milla as hardy in Virginia, and so I keep trying. Sometimes bulbs that I have failed with for years suddenly become acclimated, and bloom from then on. The only important point in the growing of these two Mexican bulbs is to remember that they need continuous summer moisture even though they must be well drained. If they are not in soil that dries out, they are easy enough for the first season. *Milla biflora,* the Mexican Star, is the only species in the genus. The inflated buds are white, striped with bright green. They open into flat, pure-white flowers, more than two and a half inches across, with segments narrowed at the base and separated like the spokes of a wheel. The pattern is as crisp and delicate as a scissor cut. In spite of the name, there are often three or more flowers to a scape. They are held far apart on pedicels six inches long, and the scapes are twelve inches or more tall. They have the heavy, exotic fragrance of cooperias. The foliage is scant, narrow, and inconspicuous.

Bessera

Bessera elegans is a related and yet very different flower, with taller, thinner scapes ending in a shower of drooping bells, red without and cream-colored within. They are called coral drops. Some authorities put this genus in milla. Corms of milla and bessera should be planted from four to six inches deep.

The Lily Family

Androstephium

Blue Bethlehem (also known as funnel-lily) is a little
flower from the southwestern prairies, related to the
brodiaeas, and very like them in appearance. It is not
breathtaking, but I like to have a few planted among
the small things that bloom in April. Its name, andro-
stephium, is from the Greek, and reflects the way the
filaments unite to form a crown. The flowers of *A.
caeruleum* are a pale French blue, crystalline and translucent. Mr. Barr sent the corms with instructions to
plant them four to five inches deep (to the base) in
very good mellow soil. "This plant thrives better for me
in part shade," he wrote, "whether on account of the
dryness of my location or its liking for shade, I do not
know. One corm next to the path, from which it gained
possibly some runoff moisture, had very much more
than the average of increase. You might not notice the
like in your garden, but in my part of the country all
things are short of moisture much of the time."

Leucocoryne

The Glory of the Sun, *Leucocoryne ixioides,* comes from
Chile, and is also called Chile-star. It blooms too early
to be planted as a summer bulb, and bulbs I have
planted in the fall have not, so far, produced any flowers the following season. However, it is a satisfactory

bulb for California and Florida. The flowers are described as sky blue with a white star in the center.

Calochortus

"Don't let anyone tell you that Mariposa tulips don't persist," Mrs. Chrismon wrote me when I asked her how they fared in Greensboro. But she means that they persist when the bulbs are taken up in summer, for our summers are too wet for them. Violet Walker made the same observation, and found that, at Woodberry, bulbs left in the ground would not survive for many seasons. So far as the winters are concerned, calochortus are perfectly hardy here, and I have read that they are hardy at least to central New York. They should be planted late—October or November—and three inches deep, in gritty, well-drained soil in light shade. Mr. Purdy recommends loose soil and leafmold, but adds that most kinds do well in heavy soils. I doubt if he knows our red clay.

The notes that Mrs. Chrismon sent me from her garden will make better reading than my sad experiences —which I attribute partly to the difference between Greensboro and Raleigh, and partly to the difference between Mrs. Chrismon and me.

"Mariposa tulips have been in bloom since March," she wrote on the third of June, "and *Calochortus venustus* is blooming now. The globe-tulips are the earliest.

This year they began to bloom at the end of March. *C. amabilis,* called Diogenes' lantern, bears little golden lamps on fifteen-inch stems; *C. albus,* the fairy lantern, is slightly taller, with lovely white flowers that last four or five days. The star-tulips began to bloom on the ninth of April. *C. Benthami* is a small one with bright yellow flowers marked with black at the base of the petals; *C. Maweanus* var. *purpurascens* and the variety *roseus* are a little larger, and carry two-inch flowers in deep purple and soft lilac pink. I had enough of these to carry the blooming season on until the latter part of May, when the charming butterfly-tulips opened. I had several forms of the variable *C. venustus.* The variety Eldorado had varicolored flowers two to four inches across; the color range includes white, pink, lilac, and purple, the whites predominating. [According to Mr. Purdy, this strain, from the Sierran foothills is among the loveliest.] The variety *citrinus* has beautiful deep yellow flowers with a black eye; the variety *oculatus* carries blossoms in white and cream, all with richly tinted eyes. *C. vesta,* the latest to bloom, is taller with flowers to four inches in diameter, flushed rose or lilac, with a broad zone of velvety brown in the center."

All of these come from California. Mr. Purdy says that *C. vesta* comes from the northwestern part of the state and grows in adobe soil. It bloomed for me in Raleigh a few times in the middle of May, but it was not at its best.

The Glory of the Snow

King, the star that shuts the even
  Calls the sheep from Tmolus down;
Home return the doves from heaven,
  And the prince to Sardis town . . .
                    A. E. Housman, "Atys"

When the chionodoxas bloom, I think of the Lydians
returning "from the hunting heavy laden" who must have
followed trails that in spring would be bordered with
these very flowers. Even in the days of Croesus they
must have been astonished at the blueness of these
flowers against the waning snowdrifts, a sight which
later moved a French botanist to call them Glory of
the Snow. These are not bulbs to be cherished as individual flowers, but they rate a doxology when planted
in quantity. And as surely as March comes around Mr.
Krippendorf gives them their due. "A plant that is
starting to self-sow, to my great joy, is *Chionodoxa
luciliae*," he wrote some years ago. "I find it everywhere,
there must be thousands. The variety *gigantea* is one of
the most beautiful of all small bulbs. I have had a few
for thirty-five years, on a hummock where a tree was
pulled up by the roots. There are never more than a
dozen or so, but the seedlings keep coming along."

The light blue-violet flowers of this variety are large
enough to cover a fifty-cent piece. They bloom in my

garden with great regularity about the tenth of March, and the type comes at the same time. Every spring I look for the bits of blue that return so faithfully in shady corners and between the roots of trees, but I have never had room to plant them as they should be planted, and as I saw them at Duke University in a solid bank of blue. There are also white and pink forms of this species, among them one called Pink Giant with large bright flowers on tall stems. None of them seem to me so desirable as the blue forms.

The gentian-blue of *C. l. sardensis* is a telling color, especially in contrast to the well-defined white star in the center. The spikes are comparatively small. In some places this species blooms early, and I have found it in flower on the ninth of February. Mr. Krippendorf says it is not persistent. "I have not planted any for thirty years," he complained, "and it has disappeared."

C. l. tmolusi is the last to bloom, and the smallest in stature, although the bright blue flowers are rather large. It needs more moisture than the others, and does best in shade. All of the others tolerate some shade, but prefer sun, and flourish in a light, well-drained loam.

Erythronium

"The western troutlilies are so little known in eastern gardens that few persons who come to visit mine have ever seen or heard of them," Mrs. Wilder wrote in *Pleasures and Problems of a Rock Garden,* nearly thirty years ago, and I still find it true. It is, as Mrs. Wilder says, a pity, for even if they do not persist—and not all of them do in this hot climate—they are very inexpensive and give great pleasure for a time, at least.

I have tried most of the western species, some of them many times, and found *Erythronium giganteum* the one that is most dependable. It grew in the Raleigh garden for nearly ten years, and bloomed regularly in late March or early April. It is not free-blooming, and usually has only one flower to a stalk. But that one is a large flower of creamy yellow with rust or red marking at the center, and delicately reflexed petals. The leaves are prettily mottled. This and *E. revolutum* like heavy, wet soils. *E. californicum* is so similar to *E. giganteum* that it was long regarded as the same species; the chief difference is that *E. californicum* has several flowers to a stem. I have never had this one, but it is generally considered the best one for the East.

One fall Mrs. Nye sent me a quantity of *E. hendersoni*. They bloomed lavishly the following spring, not so well the next season, and finally not at all. I have never had flowers that gave me more pleasure while they lasted. The pale petals are tipped with lilac, and strikingly marked with dark reddish purple. They are not so large as the yellow-flowered variety.

The most magnificent of all is *E. tuolumnense*, but it is known as a shy bloomer. After several trials a bud appeared at last, and the great golden flower opened on the third of March. That was the year when our springer,

Mr. Cayce, was a puppy. He came bounding up to the flower, looked at it with great appreciation, bit it off with one snap, and ate it with obvious relish. The large, shining leaves came up the next spring, but there were no more flowers.

The forms of *E. revolutum* are not recommended for warm climates. I tried a number of them anyway, among them *Johnsoni praecox*, Purdy's White and Pink Beauty. The last is the only one that ever blossomed, although some were planted more than once.

Our own little dogtooth violet (also called common fawn-lily), *E. americanum*, is one of the easiest wild flowers to bring in from the woods, and will bloom faithfully about the first of April. The bulbs must be dug with a long, sharp spade, for they are very deep in the soil. Mr. Starker offers several named varieties of the European species, *E. dens-canis*, including one with reddish-violet flowers, two with pink, and one pure-white form. This species is also known as dogtooth fawn-lily. According to some authorities, the picturesque but rather un-flowerlike common name is based on the resemblance of the bulb to a hound's tooth.

On the whole the erythroniums like shade and a soil rich in leafmold, and reasonably moist conditions.

Fritillaria

Of all the fritillaries I have tried, the only one that is still with me is the checkered lily, *Fritillaria meleagris*, a flower of the English meadows. It grows by the thousands in Christchurch meadows, which are often flooded by the waters of the Cherwell, and the flowers are sold "up and down the High Street in Oxford by gypsies as dark as themselves." It grows "across the Thames-side meadows rather too obviously for its own health." And it grows particularly well, Mrs. Loudon says, "near the Duke of Wellington's seat at Strathfieldsaye."

With me the handsome garden hybrids have done rather better than the wild form, whose little purple-checked bells are called snakes-heads. They bloom in my garden early in April. The most beautiful is a large silvery-white flower called Aphrodite. Various others are offered, all with classical names—Artemis, Charon, Saturnus, Orion—that sound odd when attached to these little Britishers. They are to be planted in part shade, in a damp soil in which there is plenty of leaf-mold.

I have never been able to grow any of our western fritillaries, though of course I could not resist trying them after seeing the colored pictures in Mr. Purdy's catalogue. Perhaps the soil was to blame for my failures, or maybe our climate is too hot. Mrs. Wilder speaks of the scarlet-flowered *F. recurva* as well established in rich, dark soil and shade in a garden in Westchester, and of the tiny golden bells of *F. pudica* in her own rock garden. Perhaps I should try again in Charlotte. That is one of the main troubles about writing a garden book. As you go over your notes, the flowers that have died on your hands all rise like lovely ghosts to haunt you, and fill you with an irresistible longing to try them again.

I asked Mr. Krippendorf which fritillaries he had been able to keep, and he answered that the only one still with him is *F. camtschatcensis*, which has persisted in his woods for twenty years without any attention. It grows in old gardens where it does not mind being overgrown, and must not be disturbed. But I know of no American source for bulbs of it at the present time (though Mr. Pearce offers the seed).

Hyacinthus

Like the wild hyacinth flower which on the hills
　　is found,
Which the passing feet of the shepherds for ever
　　tear and wound,
Until the purple blossom is trodden in the ground.

Sappho

When Apollo kept sheep on the hills of Thessaly, he accidentally killed the youth Hyacinthus with his discus. The god could not bring his favorite back to life, but he caused the purple hyacinth to spring up from his blood. "Everybody knows a hyacinth," Mrs. Loudon wrote a century ago, "but many of my readers will be surprised to hear that there are only three species in the genus, and that two of these are rarely seen." Although more than thirty species are now recognized, there are still very few gardeners who know that there are other hyacinths than the Dutch hybrids.

One of the earliest of the little bulbs that bloom in the rock garden is *Hyacinthus azureus*, usually listed as *Muscari azureus*. It has bloomed in my garden on the fourteenth of February, but more often it puts in an appearance the first week in March. The three-inch spikes, flaring at the base and tapering to a point like tiny porcelain pagodas, continue to rise from the ground over such a long period that I have known two months to pass between the first and the last. At first they are the gray-blue-green of an old tapestry, a color called Gobelin blue; but, as the flowers open, the color changes to a blue-violet that is called sailor blue. The delicate harmony of a patch containing these flowers in all stages, from tight, round buds to wide flaring bells, is like a page from Ridgway's color chart.

In my garden *Hyacinthus azureus* bloom faithfully for many seasons but is not given to increase. In the woods, Mr. Krippendorf says, they sow themselves by the thousands. "*H. azureus* is my darling," he once wrote on the twenty-ninth of March. "I don't know how many weeks ago I wrote you of its blueing a slope, and it still shows some color. It naturalizes easily, and as the seedlings reach blooming size the patches get bigger and thicker every year. One of them must be fifty by twenty feet. I pull some of the seeds and scatter them along the paths. In a few years these places are dotted with blue. The nicest, or at least one of the nicest, things I have seen this year is a hillside where thousands of *H. azureus* have seeded themselves, and the *Anemone apennina* and *A. blanda* that I had planted above have cross-fertilized and come up all through them in every shade from dark purple to pure white, making the bank a carpet of flowers."

When I looked up his earlier letter, I found that the first *H. azureus* of that season had bloomed in Ohio on the ninth of February along with *Scilla sibirica*. This is an earlier date than any that I have been able to record in North Carolina for either of these bulbs. There is also a variety *amphibolis*, described as a taller, later form of pale blue, with as many as fifty flowers on an eight-inch stem. All of these have smooth gray-green leaves, like those of Roman hyacinths but much smaller; they push up just ahead of the flowers, and do not last much longer. This is a great virtue, for many very small bulbs leave a lingering mass of untidy foliage behind them. The bulbs should be planted six inches deep, in gritty soil.

The alpine hyacinth, *H. amethystinus*, was brought to England from the Spanish Pyrenees in 1759, and was blooming in Mrs. Loudon's little garden in Bayswater in the summer of 1841, but, as Mrs. Wilder says, it has never been a best seller. Although Mr. Farrer called it "the most exquisite of all delights for early summer," I think he was seeing it through rosy glasses, or else he had a form superior to the one that I at last procured after many years of searching. Mine—when finally they bloomed in early May—were not a "glorious China blue." They were really white, with fine blue lines on the petals. However, they are sweet and dainty. They bring to a close the season of the small spring-flowering bulbs and come before the summer ones have well begun. The spikes of nodding bells are much like those of the small forms of *Scilla campanulata*, but the long, linear leaves are more like the foliage of the alliums. There is a pure-white form, too. This is an easy bulb to grow in the woodsy soil of a shady rock garden. I have had it for some years, and it is said to be long-lived.

Last fall I found *H. dalmaticus* offered for the first time, and this spring it bloomed in the middle of March. It is one of the tiniest and most enchanting of all the little bulbs. The little spikes are as thin as a thin pencil, and daintily tinted and delicately scented. For those who like the very tiny rock plants, this is a treasure.

Muscari

Parkinson reckoned the hyacinths as "half a hundred sorts." These evidently included the grape hyacinths, for some were "like unto little bells or stars," while others resembled "little bottles or pearls, both white and blue, sky-colored and blush." The flowers of the hyacinths are campanulate, but the flowers of the grape hyacinths are urn-shaped. Those of the common *Mus-*

cari botryoides give the genus its English name because they look like a minute bunch of blue grapes.

This species has escaped from cultivation in this country and is dear to children in spring as the roadside "blue-bottle." It is not a good bulb to plant in a small-sized garden or rock garden, for it multiplies too rapidly, and the untidy leaves come up in the fall and take up a lot of room. There are a number of forms of *botryoides*. The variety *albumis* is exquisite but cannot be counted upon to survive for many seasons. A taller, later, white grape hyacinth is offered as *M. Argaei album* (also under the species *M. szovitsianum*), and a smaller, earlier one as *M. polyanthum album*. These are equally charming, and equally impermanent. *M. botryoides* found its way from Italy to England in the sixteenth century. It usually begins to bloom early in March, but sometimes before the end of February. The light violet flowers are said to smell of ripe plums, but to me they smell like grapes in the sun.

M. armeniacum is sometimes called the early giant, but it blooms later in March. The spikes are taller (to eight inches) and larger than those of *M. botryoides*, and the flowers are deep chicory blue. The early giant, or Armenian grape hyacinth, blooms for a very long time, at least six weeks, and makes a nice patch of blue near the pale yellow rock-garden daffodils.

M. racemosum is a small species with dark blue flowers, native to Europe and Asia, and found wild in England and in this country. Mrs. Loudon called it (and many still call it) the starch hyacinth, because, she says, the flowers smell of wet starch.

The wide solitary leaves of M. *latifolium* come up wrapped around the flower spikes and pinched together at the top to form little hoods. The sterile flowers at the top are pale blue, and those beneath are a very dark blue. This species blooms early in April.

The tassel hyacinth, M. *comosum*, blooms the last of all, at the end of April. It is not pretty. The dull spikes are tinged purple, yellow-green, and olive, and they grow to nearly a foot in height. The feather hyacinth of old southern gardens is a form of M. *comosum*, usually listed as the variety *monstrosum* or *plumosum*. It once grew at Monticello. The flowers are shredded, and translucent as blue glass.

The musk grape hyacinth, M. *moschatum*, must be the oldest muscari in cultivation, for according to Mrs. Loudon it was brought out from Constantinople in 1554. The musk-scented flowers are supposed to have given the genus its name. They are purple at first, changing to greenish yellow. There is also a variety *flavum*, which Mrs. Loudon said is "a great favorite with the Turkish girls, as in the language of flowers it signifies their assent to their lovers' entreaties."

Nothoscordum

This is a small genus, not much noticed by gardeners and horticulturalists, but very acceptable to me. I like the humble flowers. The name is from the Greek, meaning false garlic, and the genus is commonly so called because it is related to the alliums; but the narrow basal leaves do not have the onion odor. The flowers, like those of the alliums, are small and starry, and in many-flowered umbels on bare scapes.

Dr. Totten identified as *Nothoscordum fragrans* a small bulb that Mrs. Boggs sent to me from St. Philip's churchyard in Charleston. "The blossoms are sweeter than pinks," she wrote, "and there are millions of them in March." With me they bloom at the end of April, and often repeat in midsummer. The second blooming is better than the first. I was disappointed that the bulbs did not increase lavishly and immediately, but I suppose that at St. Philip's they have been at it for a long time, and they may yet become a nuisance in my garden. The flowers are small and white, eight to twenty to an umbel, on a sixteen-inch scape. The pale green strap-like leaves, less than half an inch wide, and rather lax, are shorter than the scapes.

Some years ago I acquired from a California dealer a small bulb under the name of *Ornithogalum gramineum* to which I could find no reference until I came upon it accidentally (in the Weather's *Bulb Book*) as a synonym of *Nothoscordum striatellum*. Weathers dismisses the species with the remark that it has greenish-yellow flowers—which with me it has not—but I find that white flowers are often described in that way, especially if they have a yellow center.

In California it blooms all winter and into the spring. Here it begins in late March, and blooms for some weeks before taking a summer siesta. In September and October more buds appear and, ignoring the frost, continue to open until Christmas. The small, white, allium-like flowers are in umbels of six or eight, on ten-inch scapes which stand stiffly among the narrow, bright green leaves. The leaves are very much like those of *N. fragrans,* but not much more than half as wide. They persist throughout the year. To me this is a delightfully dainty and airy flower with many good traits and no bad ones. Once established, the bulbs take care of themselves, and increase slowly. Mine are in a light, poor soil in full sun, and it may be that they would relish a richer diet.

In the Royal Horticultural Society's *Dictionary of Gardening, N. striatellum* is given as a variety of *N. striatum,* which in this country is known as *N. bivalve,* a native of the southern states and Mexico. In Texas it grows along railroad rights-of-way, in lawns, vacant lots, roadside ditches, and mesquite flats . . . and is so common that its good qualities have been overlooked. The lack of appreciation given to it is shown by its common names—"False Garlic" and "Crow Poison." Beginning to bloom with the first spring flowers, it continues until summer, and then after a brief interval blooms again in the fall. Umbels of fragrant white or cream-colored flowers are borne on short, delicate stems above the narrow, grassy leaves. As is to be expected from a bulb so widely distributed, there are numerous forms, some with larger flowers than others, and I expect its garden value depends upon the form. It grows either in sand or clay. In *The Fragrant Path*, Mrs. Wilder says that *N. bivalve* was hardy in her garden, and "very pretty in a modest way."

Trillium

"For the beginner in growing wild flowers," George D. Aiken says, "there is hardly a family more satisfactory than the trilliums." [4] It does not seem to me that they are for the beginner. To my mind they are an acquired taste, and not so easy to grow. As far back as I can remember anything, I remember the delight of rediscovering each spring the quaint faces of bird's-foot violets, the furry buds of hepaticas, and the ineffable fragrance of arbutus; but a passion for trilliums grows slowly. Only long acquaintance has made me aware of the insistent rhythm of three in this plant, repeated in the leaves, sepals, petals, and carpels; and of the rich colors of the flowers, and of the variety in the patterns of the foliage.

Trilliums—wake-robins—require shade and a soil that is deeply dug and rich in leafmold. It is important to move the tubers only in late summer or early fall when the tops have died away, and to replant them as soon as possible, four inches deep. I find them slow to recover

[4] *Pioneering with Wild Flowers.* Putney, Vermont, 1933.

after transplanting, and apt not to bloom for a season or two, but once established they are there forever. Except for a yearly mulch of rotted leaves they should be left undisturbed.

"I think the biggest thrill I have had this year was finding *Trillium nivale*," Mr. Krippendorf wrote on the ninth of May. "About ten years ago I collected a few plants in the dolomite country, fifty miles east of us, on the single hillside where it is really plentiful. I thought it had disappeared years ago, but last Sunday I found this perfect clump."

The snow trillium is one that refused to grow in my garden, either because of the heat, or because of the soil's acidity. As it has a preference for dryish neutral soils, Dr. Wherry [5] recommends it especially for limestone rock gardens. *T. nivale* is a tiny one, only four inches high, with a pure-white flower. It is called the snow trillium more because of its earliness than its whiteness, for in New England it is the first to bloom, often pushing up through the snow.

The species with sessile flowers are many, especially in the South. *T. sessile*, called the toad trillium because of the brown mottling on the leaves, is found in woods along the Potomac and westward to Minnesota. This is not one of the showy ones, for the flowers are small, dark, and insignificant. *T. luteum*, a rare form of *T. sessile*, found only in North Carolina and Tennessee, occurs in the foothills as well as in the mountains, and will

[5] *Wild Flower Guide.* New York, Doubleday, 1948.

grow at low elevations. It is one of the easiest in cultivation, and seems indifferent to soil reaction. It blooms
with me between early and mid-April, and the flowers
are fresh for nearly three weeks. This long-lasting quality is one of the good characteristics of trilliums. The
three green sepals lie flat on wide gray and green leaves,
and the three citron-yellow petals stand erect and close
together like a candle flame. The stalks vary in height,
but in my garden they reach about ten inches.

T. discolor is always dwarf; the plants grow close together, covering the ground. One of the rarest trilliums,
it is found only, Mr. Clement says, along the Savannah
River and its tributaries, whether in the mountains or
the piedmont. The round leaves are mottled in a flickering pattern of two shades of gray; the green sepals are
flat, and the cream-colored petals are erect.

The whippoorwill flower, *T. hugeri,* occurs in rich
woods from North Carolina to Florida. It is a giant species; its flowers are usually dark red, although they may
be yellow or green. In other respects it is similar to *T.
luteum.* The most spectacular of all trilliums, and one
of the first to flower, is *T. underwoodi.* I found it in
bloom in Chapel Hill in late March, and Mrs. Henry
says that it blooms in Pennsylvania in mid-April. It
grows in ferny woods from North Carolina and Tennessee to Florida and Alabama, and Mrs. Totten says hers
came from Florida. In Chapel Hill it never increased,
although it bloomed every spring, but Mrs. Henry says
that with her it is an excellent grower, and self-sows

freely. The dark flowers smell of musk. The crimson petals are erect; the flat sepals are mottled with olive green. The vivid pattern of the leaves is a combination of pale gray, bright green, and dark green. This is usually a dwarf species, not over eight inches tall, but the flowers and leaves are large in proportion.

The purple trillium, *T. ludovicianum,* is a similar species from Mississippi and Louisiana. Miss Dormon says that it grows in the woods with jack-in-the-pulpit and mandrake. *T. stamineum,* of the rocky woods from Georgia to Mississippi, is another species with dark, sessile flowers and mottled leaves. The plant is like that of *T. hugeri,* but on a smaller scale.

"Yesterday evening I walked down to the brook again," Mr. Krippendorf wrote late in April. "The little flat on the other side is in full bloom, carpeted with phlox, white violets, and the starry chickweed. Lots of nodding trilliums (ranging from deep chocolate to purest white) are in bloom on the slopes with Canada violets and celandine poppies."

A slope is a good place for the nodding wake-robins, *T. cernuum.* If they are planted on level ground you have either to pick the flowers or stand on your head in order to see them. In my garden the flowers come out shell pink, and grow rosy with age. They are delicate and delicately scented, with crystalline petals that are sharply recurved, and curled at the tips. This species grows a foot or more tall in moist places, but in a dry part of my rock garden the dark stalks are only seven inches tall. It comes into bloom between the first and last weeks of April, and may be found in the woods all the way from Canada to Georgia.

The southern, or rose trillium, *T. stylosum,* and the sweet trillium, *T. vaseyi,* occur only from North Carolina to Georgia, and mostly in the mountains. (Mr. Clement says that the bashful wake-robin, *T. catesbaei,* which occurs in the piedmont, is the same species as *T. stylosum.*) I first saw the southern trillium in Mr. Harlowe's wonderful garden in the Poconos, where it was in bloom the last week in May, the last species to flower. In the South it comes at the end of April or early in May. It is small and frail, or tall and sturdy, according to the kind of soil in which it grows, for all trilliums respond like magic to humus and moisture in the soil. The petals of the flowers are narrow and curved backward, and of a pale amaranth pink. They are crisped at the margins.

T. vaseyi is sometimes called sweet Beth, which has a modest and feminine sound, but the flower is the giant of the genus, and is said to be sometimes six inches across. The plants grow to two feet tall. The most enormous one that I have ever seen was growing above the stream in the Knights' garden in Biltmore Forest. The crimson velvet flower beneath the wide leaves was as close to fantastic as anything could seem in those dimly lit, fairy-tale woods where the ground beneath the hemlocks is carpeted with galax and wintergreen, and the air is scented by strange shrubs brought there from Florida. Even the ordinary jack-in-the-pulpit takes on heroic size and tropical plumage, and appears in startlingly distinct stripes of white and bright green, with a bright purple stem. Crimson or a red-brown is the common color of the flowers of *T. vaseyi,* but they are found in all sorts of lovely and subtle tones from deep purple to pale pink. Mr. Clement showed me a rare white form which he had found along the Tuckasegee River.

T. grandiflorum, a large-flowered wake-robin, belonging to that group of trilliums with flowers on erect pedicels, occurs in northern woods, and ranges this far south only in the mountains. Dr. Wherry says that it is the easiest to bring into the garden, but that the painted trillium, *T. undulatum,* "requires greater acidity and summer coolness than the average rock gardener can supply, so it had better be left in the woods." I could never get either of these established in Raleigh, but I have seen the painted trillium in bloom in Miss Isabel Busbee's garden, where the wide white blossoms, splashed with raspberry, were delightfully conspicuous in a dark, damp bed of ferns beneath some shrubs.

The ill-scented wake-robin, *T. erectum,* is another northern species that comes down into our mountains. This one grows easily in Raleigh, and blooms in April. Unless my nose deceives me, it is not at all ill-scented. The flowers are small and neat, and have narrow, pointed segments. The petals are of that dark, bright red-violet that is called burnt lake. They are a smart contrast to the apple-green sepals, but each sepal has a central hairline of maroon which brings the design together. There is an albino form, called the wax trillium, with dead-white petals, pale green sepals, and dark red anthers. The pedicels of the flowers of this species are usually erect, as the Latin name implies, but sometimes curve downward so that the flowers are hidden beneath the leaves. This confused me for a long time, until Mr. Clement assured me that a plant with a curved pedicel could still be *T. erectum.* "Not that the botanists will agree," he added darkly, his blue eyes on the blue mountains, and the most wonderful collection of trilliums that I have ever seen spread out in bloom at his feet.

T. pusillum is a not-much-prized species found only in the pinelands of the coastal plain in southern Virginia and the Carolinas. Like *T. erectum* it is low-growing. The flowers are white or pink.

The showiest southern trillium of this group is the very rare and hard-to-come-by *T. simile,* found only in the mountains and the piedmont of Georgia and the Carolinas. It is a giant plant, to two feet tall, and the large white flowers, held well above the leaves on their long pedicels, are made even more striking by the dark ovary. I have never been so fortunate as to possess this species, but I have read somewhere that, once established, it self-sows freely.

The Wild Tulips

The tulip species are many, but their season is not long. All the brilliance and gaiety of their blossoming are crowded into the weeks between early March and early May. Two at least, the lady tulip and the wood tulip, have been in cultivation in the South since the eighteenth century (or thereabouts), for Thomas Jefferson had both at Monticello. If we had more modern gardeners with the eighteenth-century curiosity, we would soon learn which of the other species will thrive in the southern states and which will not. I have tried a number myself, but since until recently only a few have been available, I have not records for as many, or for as long a period, as I would like.

They say that you had best take up your tulips if it rains on Saint Swithin's Day, for six weeks of wet weather are sure to follow. Last July Saint Swithin did his worst, but I left the little bulbs in the ground as usual. This spring the bloom was as satisfactory as ever.

Species tulips come from Mediterranean and oriental countries where the summers are not only hot but very dry. Thus it is probable that I would have better luck with them if I lifted the dormant bulbs and stored them in the intense heat of the attic (not in the cool, damp cellar), but such pampering is a bit too much trouble for me. I simply plant the bulbs in light, rich, and limy soil, in raised beds where they get maximum sun. I keep the foliage of nearby plants from overshadowing them, and I keep the hose away from the places where they are planted. Then, if they remain, I welcome the flowers joyfully, and if they depart, I sigh and try again.

The year I began my new garden in Charlotte, Mr. Moody sent me a collection of forty different botanical tulips and hybrids, which gave me a chance to check, in a new place, those that I had grown in Raleigh. Although they were not planted until the middle of January, the late planting did not seem to hurt them, and did not affect the time of bloom. On the whole I found that the ones that had been satisfactory before were successful here; and those that had been uncertain were still uncertain.

I sent notes on all of the species that I have grown to the American Rock Garden Society, and later Alida Livingston added her experiences with botanical tulips on Long Island.[6]

"My tulips," she writes, "live on an exposed terrace which I dug out of a gravel bank for them in an effort to simulate one of those dreary Near-East pastures where goats thrive and cows do not venture. In the excavation, about three feet deep, some of the gravel remained behind. Larger stones were added, plus a fairly substantial mixture of clay loam and leafmold. This terrace catches the autumn rains and all the snow the winter may bring. In spring it is decidedly moist, in summer

[6] *Bulletin of the American Rock Garden Society*. Vol. 9, No. 5, pp. 74-76.

baked dry. The tulips are planted deep, not less than six inches, sometimes more than eight inches, regardless of the fact that the bulbs are usually small."

In Charlotte, my tulips (as they were in Raleigh) are planted at the top of a retaining wall of stones laid without cement. The soil is just what was there, loam or heavy clay, most of it very bad. I mixed in leafmold, bonemeal, and sand as I planted. I always plant all bulbs very shallowly, as it is less trouble, and I comfort myself with the thought that if they make themselves at home they will dig in to the depth they like. Our soil is always moist in spring, and sometimes very wet in summer.

When I started to collect the little tulips I searched particularly for the early-blooming kinds, for where spring comes early the early flowers are especially dear, but these often proved to be the most uncertain species because the buds may be nipped before they bloom. One year the first was *Tulipa biflora,* the smallest of all— so small that when I told my mother that one was out, she went to look for it and came back and said indignantly that there was nothing there. However, the patch is clearly visible when in full bloom. There are usually two flowers to a stem, but there may be more. The flowers must be variable, for no two descriptions are alike. The ones I had were creamy white inside and vinaceous outside. They started blooming close to the ground on the twenty-third of March, and they looked at first like very small crocuses. Later the stems reached three or four inches, and the two pale, long-tapered leaves stretched up to six inches. *T. biflora* bloomed beautifully the first season, but that was the end, and a second trial was even less successful. It is a difficult species at best—Mrs. Wilder said that it was not permanent with her—and since it comes from the Russian steppes it may never be taught to survive our too-hot summers and not-cold-enough winters. Still, it is one of the flowers that take possession of memory, and if patience and attention to its needs can make it grow I shall succeed eventually.

I came off no better with the variety *turkestanica,* a taller, more vigorous, and later-blooming form of *T. biflora,* but I have had it only once. It is rampant on Long Island, "perhaps because I do not like it much," Mrs. Livingston adds, "it reminds me of star of Bethlehem, and I am not very fond of any ornithogalum."

T. dasystemon, also from Turkestan, and with several flowers to a stem, is another that often blooms too early with me. Mr. Krippendorf wrote: "I wish I had some place where I could grow it well. It is a lovely thing." On Long Island it is "very satisfactory, producing its pretty yellow and white flowers abundantly while also increasing steadily."

Mrs. Livingston notes that "for two years, at least, *T. pulchella* has given an excellent account of itself, sometimes sending two stems from one bulb. The relatively large flowers are rather variable in color, some almost violet and some a royal purple, all pleasing, none magenta." One year in Raleigh this was my earliest tulip, blooming in mid-March, but I could never keep it for as long as two years, there or in Charlotte. It is the most brilliant of all the species tulips, and I know of no other bulb that makes such a splash in the rock garden so early in the season except *Sisyrinchium Douglasi*, the grass widow. This silken flower from the moist slopes of the Pacific Northwest is fugitive, too, and I judge that it is generally difficult in culture, for it has been dropped from the lists of the western dealers from whom I used to get it. I liked it for the sake of its purple splendor at the end of February. *T. pulchella* is a tiny replica of a Darwin tulip with a two-inch stem and glaucous leaves about five inches long. *T. violacea's* flowers are solferino purple. The center is a wonderful golden brown with a narrow rim of gold, and the dark anthers are covered with dull gold pollen.

Usually the waterlily tulip in one of its forms is the first to bloom, but these handsome modern hybrids are too large and too gaudy to associate with the smaller species. The typical *T. kaufmanniana* with its shallow cups of carmine and cream is now available in a multitude of colors. The earliest date that I have for this group is for the variety *solanus* on March second. From then on they bloom in succession for several weeks, ending with the variety Henriette at the end of March or in April. The last, one of the most beautiful, is ivory-white marked with rose. The variety Fritz Kreisler is early and one of the most striking. The inside of the large flowers is like peaches and cream, and the outside is almost pure pink with just a touch of violet.

T. clusiana, the lady tulip, often blooms in the middle of March. This is dainty but not small. In good soil the stems may grow to eighteen inches. Still, it has a delicate air, and looks better among rocks than in the border. South of Washington the lady tulip is the most dependable species for blooming, enduring, and increasing (I have read that it does not set seed but travels by stolons—anyway, it is always coming up in a delightful and mysterious ways in odd places). But it is uncertain in northern gardens. The lovely pointed buds, striped red and white like peppermint candy, open only in the sun, but they are decorative even when closed up tight. Within, the flowers are creamy except for a disk of dahlia carmine in the center. They are very fragrant.

Mrs. Loudon finds the starry tulip, *T. stellata,* "so unlike most other tulips as to be scarcely recognizable as belonging to that genus. It is remarkable for its starlike appearance, occasioned by the narrowness of the segments of its perianth, and their spreading out almost flat when the sun shines, although they close again in the evening." In spite of its unique appearance when wide open, this Himalayan species is so similar to its near relative, the lady tulip, that, especially as they bloom about the same time, no one but a collector would want both of them. *T. primulina,* an Algerian relative of the lady tulip, is not available at present to my knowledge, but Mrs. Wilder praises it as a most willing and reliable sort. It is white within, and green without, and has the strange habit of closing instead of opening in the heat of the day.

The wood tulip, *T. sylvestris,* is one of the early ones, blooming for me sometimes before the middle of March. This graceful and fragrant flower is an old favorite in gardens, and is easily grown. "Once planted," Mrs. Loudon says, "it requires no further care. We have two or three bulbs, which were sent to Mr. Loudon about twelve years ago from France, and which have flowered freely every year without being taken up, or, in short, anything being done to them." I am very glad to hear that Mr. Loudon was a gardener in his own right, and so well thought of on the Continent as to have tulip bulbs sent to him. I cannot remember his having been mentioned elsewhere in his wife's writings, and until I came upon this passage I had pictured him as a middle-class merchant with no appreciation of flowers. I do hope he admired the bulbs before he planted them, for they are as beautiful as flowers—small, smooth, and pointed, and of a soft orange color. Strange to say, the typical wood tulip has a bad reputation as to flowering in this country. I have reports from Alabama and New York that after blooming for a few years it sends up leaves without flowers, and I have had the same experience in North Carolina. It is worth taking trouble to find the less common but much more free-flowering variety *major,* which is "out to possess the earth. It

sends stolons in every direction and blooms with abandon, trying to masquerade as a field of golden daffodils."

Another European species, *T. australis*, is closely related to the wood tulip. The fragrant flowers are of the
same bright yellow, and have the same habit of closing
at night and opening only after ten o'clock in the morning, or even later in the day if it is at all cloudy. The
slender, pointed buds, tinged with red and green, are as
decorative as the flowers. I wonder why this delightful
tulip is so uncommon. I have had it only once, when it
bloomed early in April, and have never been able to
find it again.

I must mention one more early-blooming tulip, *T.*
saxatilis, although only to say that that seems to be a
universal failure. "It sends up a large, flapping green
leaf in winter and nothing more," Mrs. Livingston says.
"It hasn't even the grace to disappear." I have tried it a
number of times, both here and in Raleigh, and have
never had a blossom.

In these parts, the species that bloom late seem on
the whole to be the most reliable. Two very small ones
that have done well with me bloom in mid-April or a
little earlier. *T. batalini* is native to Bokhara. It produces milky-yellow flowers, aureolin yellow within,
paler without, and with smoothness of texture and
delicacy of outline that seem to be peculiar to very
small flowers. The urn-shaped buds are like the tulips in
old prints. They stand about six inches above the pale,
red-rimmed leaves. *T. aucheriana*, from the Near East,

has the same delicacy of color and line. In full sun the mallow-pink flowers open into silver-centered stars that seem to rest on the long, tapered, gray leaves. On Long Island this species increases rapidly, but it has not done so with me; which is unfortunate, for it is one of the few expensive ones, and is seldom offered.

T. chrysantha is another Persian species that seems in general to respond to cultivation in this country. Mr. Berry reports that this and the lady tulip are the most persistent sorts in southern California. Mrs. Livingston writes that *T. chrysantha* flourishes with her, perhaps on account of the summer heat, and "blooms most regularly. The five or six original bulbs have increased to over fifty." It was still growing in my Raleigh garden when I left, blooming about the middle of April, and lasting for two weeks. I do not remember that I took any pains with it, but it might be as well to plant the bulbs six to eight inches deep, give them perfect drainage, and provide a cushion of sand. The lemon-colored flowers come in pairs and open late in the day, sometimes not until afternoon. They are sweet-smelling, with a fresh, delicate fragrance that is hard to define.

T. hageri has proved one of the easiest and best, both here and in Raleigh. It blooms regularly in early April, the original clump increasing in girth, and flowering more freely each year. The flower is a cylix, and of a dark rich red that makes the clear primary colors of spring seem garish and crude. The color is not in Ridgway (although not far from nopal red). *T. hageri* re-

minds me of old tiles, or of the soft orange of Pompeian
frescoes. The anthers are a dull plum color when the
flower opens, and then they split and turn out a coat of
rust-colored pollen. The bright green buds, slowly turning red, and the narrow curled leaves, are a part of the
pattern. I wondered where I would put such a flower,
if I had a choice, for in my shady garden there is little
choice for plants that must have their place in the sun.
I wandered about the garden in search of harmonious
colors. The difficulty is that, in our interrupted springs,
flowers that bloom together one year may miss each
other the next. This tulip would be charming with wild
columbine, but in any given season the columbine might
open too late. I wish I had a rocky path where full sun
shifted hour by hour and inch by inch into shade, and
where I could plant dull red and dull orange flowers
with flowers of old gold. I would like to plant *T. hageri*
between those rusty-brown sandhill rocks which (Mr.
Maurice tells me) are called triassic sandstone. Wild
columbine would be in the background (whether it
blooms at the same time or not), plus clumps of the
fulvous Louisiana irises. Beyond these I would like the
rare *Azalea austrina* and a Japanese quince that grows
little above a foot in height and carries a scattering of
terra-cotta flowers most of the year.

This April I had in bloom, for the first time, a much
tinier red tulip, another species from Bokhara, *T. lini-
folia*, with scarlet petals and narrow, gray, wavy-edged
leaves that lie flat on the ground. The contrast between

the intensity of the color and the minuteness of the blossom kept my thoughts returning to it all summer.

T. marjoletti, from Savoy, is graceful enough for the rock garden, but the slender stems reach a height of eighteen inches, and the flowers are proportionately large. The flowers are the shape of the garden tulips, not opening wide, but remaining prim little globes. When they first color they are citron yellow with a faint tinge of red on the outside of the petals; as the flowers mature they become cream color, and the splashes of red grow deeper and wider. Everything about this tulip is subtle and elegant: the form, the coloring, and the strange perfume that smells of "sugar and spice and everything nice." It has bloomed with me a second April, and I hope that it will become a fixture.

I first saw *T. patens,* better known to gardeners as *T. persica,* in Mr. Harlowe's garden in the Poconos, where it was the last species of the season, blooming at the end of May. With me it blooms among the early ones at the end of March, a little flower in cloisonné, with an indefinable scent that becomes more intense when the flower is picked. The buds are of vinaceous orange, and never open wide, even when the sun is full upon them. The sepals are slightly reflexed, and the petals part just enough to show the clear, lemon-yellow interior.

The last to bloom is *T. sprengeri,* an Armenian species, tall but graceful, with large flowers on twelve-inch stems. The flowers are greenish yellow in the bud, and the intense color called signal red within. Mrs. Wilder reported this tulip as blooming in New York in mid-June. It bloomed for me the first of May, and had bloomed only once when I left Raleigh. With Mrs. Livingston it is very persistent, but does not increase readily. I read somewhere that the bulbs should be put into the ground as soon as they arrive.

I had no luck with *T. urumiensis,* a species from Asia Minor, but I have tried it only once, and Mrs. Livingston says that it is "neither rare, expensive, nor difficult. It looks like a yellow *T. dasystemon,* and is a little taller."

The horned tulip, *T. acuminata,* is of unknown origin but is called the Turkish tulip. It blooms in mid-April. The curious flowers, with tapered ribbonlike petals five inches long, are currant-red streaked with pale yellow. They are more interesting than beautiful, and I am not at all distressed that this species has never flourished in my garden.

T. praecox from Central Europe has not lived up to its name or its reputation for early flowers, but blooms after the middle of March. The Asiatic *T. eichleri* and *T. praestans* from Bokhara bloom about the same time. These three bright red tulips of medium size have prospered in North Carolina. They should be planted by themselves with thyme and santolina where they will not outshine the daintier species.

These are the botanical tulips that I know. Several

other species are available at the present time, and I should like to try them all. I like to think, as each spring comes around, that a new tulip will be in bloom in the rock garden.

10

Some Amaryllids

Amaryllis

The little bulbs in this genus (and the big ones, too) have been and still are involved in more than their share of confusion in plant nomenclature. The oxblood lily, *Amaryllis advena* (*Hippeastrum advenum* in *Hortus Second*), has borne many labels since Herbert gave it the lovely name *Habranthus hesperius*. (Mr. Giridlian now lists it as *Rhodophiala gifida*.) It was as a habranthus that it first came to me from

Mr. Hall's garden in Texas, and it is by that name that it is best known to gardeners. It is the easiest to grow, and one of the hardiest of the small amaryllids. Dr. Traub reports that it is hardy in Beltsville, Maryland, and Mr. Houdyshel recommends it for trial in Pennsylvania, Ohio (although I have never found any enthusiasm for it in Ohio), Indiana, Missouri, and southern Kansas. It seems to grow equally well in all parts of the South, and in my garden it has bloomed for years, with regularity and in profusion, from the middle or end of August through September and into October.

The drooping flowers, usually five to seven on a ten-inch scape, never open wide. The narrow, pointed petals are a strange dark red, between oxblood and carmine, that glows and sparkles like semi-precious stones. The flowers open several at a time, and do not last long, because the texture of the petals is so delicate. They are scentless. The narrow, red-flecked, shiny leaves come up with the flowers, but develop later and stay fresh all winter.

The best time to move the bulbs is in July when the foliage has died away, but I think it can be done safely at any time. They will bloom the same season if planted before the first of October. The bulbs are small and round with a long neck. I plant them so that the top of the neck is just above the soil, but when I dig them out they usually have worked themselves down to a depth that is more than the length of a garden spade. They grow in any soil, but bloom for me only in the open.

Some Amaryllids

A pink form is available, but it does not bloom so
freely, and it increases very slowly. The color is daphne
red which is much grayed red-violet, and looks well
with the foliage of gray-leaved plants. There is a yellow
form, too, which Mr. Giridlian now lists. Mrs. Loudon
says that it is hardier than the type, and I have a note
as to its being hardy in New York. The flowers are of a
"pale lemon color."

Chlidanthus

The deep-rooted satisfaction of bringing to bloom a
never-seen but long-imagined flower comes, upon occasion, to the gardener who collects rare bulbs. I must
have desired *Chlidanthus fragrans* for nearly a score of
years before I had this satisfaction, and I cannot remember during how many seasons, nor in what soils
and situations, I had planted the bulbs, before I decided to try once more. I was promptly rewarded for
my perseverance. I planted two bulbs one early May,
and a week or ten days later they bloomed. They came
up, like the rain lilies to which they are close kin, after
the first hard rain, and they bloomed with a radiance
that seemed to me to light up all the garden. This is the
kind of experience that makes me such a careless gardener. I have read a lot about the culture of this difficult bulb, and I have taken it all to heart. Some say that
it will bloom only when the clumps are crowded into
pots, others that they must be divided each season.

Some say that the bulbs must be left undisturbed, and some that they must be lifted and dried, but I have had ample proof that they will bloom when they are ready to, and that nothing I can do will make them hurry. It is safe to state that *C. fragrans* is hardy in North Carolina—for I find the foliage coming back year after year —and that the bulbs will not bloom if left in the ground, for they must be lifted, even in southern California. They can be stored over winter (divided or undivided) in dry sand, and at least there is a chance that they will bloom when they are set out in the spring.

The name *chlidanthus* means delicate flower. The flowers are like golden rain lilies, except that, instead of being solitary, they are borne two or three or four to a stem. When the bulbs are planted in the spring the scapes come up first, and the leaves follow. In spite of being called *fragrans,* and in spite of Mrs. Loudon's statement that their perfume has been compared to frankincense, I find the flowers almost scentless. This species grows in the Andes. The English writers speak of a Mexican species, or perhaps only a variety, *C. ehrenbergi,* from Mexico. This is not to be found in the American trade, but I wish I might obtain it, for I have an idea that here it might do better than the South American one.

Cyanella

This is a name new to me, as well as to many botanical authorities. It does not appear in *Hortus Second,* so the genus apparently has not been in recent cultivation in this country. Mrs. Loudon, however, grew three species which were not new even in her day. She describes *Cyanella capensis* as a very elegant plant with a purple flower something like a small ixia, and *C. lutea* (also a Cape bulb) as so different that it does not seem to belong to the same genus. *C. capensis* did not survive the winter in my garden, but *C. lutea* bloomed this spring on the tenth of May. The flower is not like any that I know—except, perhaps, a small pale orchid. The perianth, with its six segments forming two triangles, one within the other, is a slightly grayed citron with fine olive lines on the reverse. Five stamens with lemon-yellow anthers form a little hood from which hangs the sixth stamen and the style. The individual flowers last two or three days and, as Mrs. Loudon observed, "they continue for several weeks in succession." I was amazed to find them still in bloom when I returned at the end of June from a three-week trip. The wiry nine-inch stems continue to branch, and the branches continue to bloom. As soon as the flowers have faded the tufts of narrow leaves vanish. If there were any seeds, I did not see them.

C. lutea needs a very rich, sandy soil in full sun. It is considered to be as hardy as an ixia, and I hope it will live to bloom another year, but I shall take no chances, for I cannot let next spring go by without another look at the intricacies of this small flower. Mr. Giridlian also lists *C. orchidiformis*. Quite distinct from *C. capensis*, it bears "hundreds of orchid-like flowers on tall, well-branched stems."

Cyrtanthus

The Ifafa lilies are small amaryllids from South Africa with curved tubular flowers, several to an umbel. In this country they are grown mostly in California; of those that I have had from the western dealers, none has persisted. Mr. James writes in *Herbertia* that they need sun in winter, and plenty of water, but that good drainage is essential. Thus my failure may have been due to my notion that cyrtanthus would like the low, moist place where the zephyr lilies grow. I mean to try them again in drier, sunnier parts of the garden, and in light soil.

C. angustifolius is said to be the hardiest, but I have never found it listed in the trade. It is called the fire lily because the red flowers spring up on their native hills after the grass has been burned in August. *C. ochroleucus* and *C. parviflorus* are the only ones that have flowered for me. Both bloomed in the middle of May from bulbs planted in April. The first is called the white Ifafa lily, but the pale flowers are really empire yellow. There are two or three to an umbel, and they are fragrant. The scarlet flowers of *C. parviflorus* are smaller, but there are more to an umbel. In California, *C. ochroleucus* blooms in winter and *C. parviflorus* in early spring. I have had the white-flowered *C. mackeni* twice but it has not bloomed. This grows in swamps in Natal, so the zephyr lily spot should have suited it.

Ixiolirion

Because blue is a rare color in the amaryllis family, the ixia lily is of especial interest in a collection of small amaryllids. The flowers are like frilly brodiaeas, and of the deep blue that is called Bradley's violet. They bloom here at the very end of April. Although Mrs. Wilder speaks of it as hardy wherever tulips are hardy, this bulb has never persisted with me. I think the reason for this is our wet winters, for the bulbs are dormant then, and that is the very time they should be kept as dry as possible. Several species are offered in the trade, but they all seem to be forms of *Ixiolirion montanum* which has a wide range from Siberia to western Asia.

Sternbergia

Mr. Krippendorf has written of finding sternbergia in bloom early in September, although he says that it does not really thrive in Ohio. By not thriving he probably means that it has failed to carpet the woods with flowers. It is a temperamental bulb even in more favorable climates. I have read that bloom is more a matter of lime than of latitude (for in the Mediterranean region, the bulbs are generally found on limestone), but I think the truth is that, like some other amaryllids, it is apt to miss flowering for a season, and nothing the gardener can do or leave undone is likely to help or hinder. As to hardiness, Elizabeth Rawlinson said that bulbs in her garden in Staunton were unharmed by fifteen degrees below zero, and that others had wintered at the Gardiner Museum in Boston, and in Wellesley, and in Connecticut.

Sternbergia lutea, the only species much known in gardens, has been called winter daffodil, fall crocus, and yellow amaryllis, but still has no widely popular name. A native of Palestine, Syria, and Persia, this is one of the many flowers identified as the biblical Lily of the Field, and it may well have surpassed Solomon in all his glory, for the radiant flowers are pure gold. They have bloomed in Virginia gardens for many generations, and according to tradition grew in the Palace Gardens at Williamsburg in colonial times. For a time these old gardens were about the only source for the bulbs, but now most dealers list them, and send them out in late summer. They will bloom even when planted in September. The books tell you to plant the long-necked bulbs six inches deep, but I have an idea that they bloom better if barely covered, for once I found some lying on top of the compost heap with no soil at all, and they were smothered with flowers. Then they tell you that a summer baking is essential, but the most brilliant patch I ever saw was under a great live oak in Tarboro, North Carolina. In Raleigh, too, they bloomed freely under the oak trees, and most freely of all after one of the wettest summers I have known. The flowers are like crocuses in form, and like buttercups in color and substance. Since frost does not spoil them, the last are as perfect as the first, even when they bloom—as they sometimes do—at the end of October. The variety *angustifolia* is the best of the numerous forms, a late bloomer and more free-flowering than the type.

I gather that S. *macrantha* is the most desirable of the other species. Its provenance in the mountains of Asia Minor gives it the advantage of extra hardiness, and its habit of producing foliage in spring, when it is less likely to be injured by frost, instead of in fall, makes it more certain to flower. Also, it blooms later, and may continue into December. Unfortunately, it is extremely rare.

The Rain Lilies

Cooperia, habranthus, and zephyranthes are called the rain lilies because the solitary flowers come miraculously into bloom after summer showers. I have read that after a long drought they will respond to a good watering in the same way. Dr. Alexander says that they "have proved hardy in New York, grown with the protection of a south-facing wall." [1]

For a long time the genus *habranthus* was out of favor, and the species were distributed like orphans

[1] *Addisonia,* Vol. 22, No. 3, p. 46.

among other genera. Now that it has been restored, Dr. Uphof says that there is no excuse for calling a *habranthus* a *zephyranthes*. I had been doing this very thing, but now I shall mend my ways.

HABRANTHUS

The name of this genus means delicate flower, a name very appropriate to the four species in my garden. These are hardy, persistent, and floriferous with me in North Carolina and with Miss Kell in northern Texas, and all four are available. The other seven, as described in *Herbertia,* 1946, are known only to collectors. Since all of the species come from the temperate parts of South America, I should think that there would be a good chance that they would be hardy at least to zone six, and Dr. Traub suggests that *H. juncifolia* be tried even farther north.

In 1829 Mr. Anderson collected *H. andersoni* in Montevideo, and brought it home to England, to his patron Mr. Mackey. He brought three color forms: the variety *aurea,* described as a "bright golden yellow" tone; the variety *cuprea,* a "dark copper" shade, and the variety *obscura,* a "dingy livid brown." I can see how a casual visitor to my garden, seeing this flower like a brown moth lighting on the leafmold, might think it the variety *obscura,* and consider it well named. But no one who loves color and texture could hold it in the hand without seeing that it is like a piece of rare luster. The interior is antimony yellow with a russet throat, and the exterior is a dull orange with a rosy glow and a copper sheen. The small, crocuslike flowers are held up about eight inches from the ground, and the grayish, straplike leaves are of the same length. The leaves persist throughout the year. My one bulb, which came to me from Mr. Houdyshel, has never increased, but blooms earlier each year, and for a longer period. This year it flowered first on the nineteenth of May. It does very well in the shade where I planted it, so I have left it there, although Mr. Houdyshel says that it should be in full sun. He says that it seeds itself freely, but I never let the flowers go to seed.

About the same time, Mr. Drummond collected the copper lily, *H. texanus,* sometimes considered a variety of Anderson's habranthus. This has been grown in my rock garden for more than ten years as *Zephyranthes texana.* The flowers are smaller than those of the South American species, but they have the same metallic luster. They are primuline yellow within, brick red without, tipped with deep red and tinged with serpentine green. Odorless and fleeting, they last no more than two days, and close in the afternoon. Sometimes they appear in June, with flushes in July, August, and September, and other times there is no bloom until July. The numerous, shimmering leaves are very narrow (scarcely an eighth of an inch), bright green, and flecked with red. They are practically evergreen in the moist spot where I have planted the bulbs, but in dry soil they disappear in summer. The tiny bulbs should be planted two inches deep in friable soil. This species increases little, if any, from offsets, but seeds itself freely. Mrs. Strout says she has had seedlings in bloom in two years. She says that this and *H. andersoni* do well in California, but Mr. Hayward reports that the first does not thrive in the soil of Florida. Both species are native to regions where the soil is alkaline, but in cultivation they seem not to have any preference. Both thrive with me in soil on the acid side.

H. robustus, known to some gardeners as *Zephyranthes robusta,* was introduced into England in 1827. Mrs. Loudon considered it the hardiest of all, and said it would winter in the garden if a flowerpot were turned over it in frosty weather. But, she added, if you put a flowerpot over it, it is likely to be attacked by slugs and injured by moisture, so perhaps, after all, it is better to follow Mr. Herbert's advice and winter it in the greenhouse. Fortunately the North Carolina gardener has none of these problems. Here you put the bulbs in the ground, and enjoy them forever after. This seems to be generally true in the Southeast, and from Florida to southern California, but Mrs. Strout reports that it does not thrive near San Francisco.

In my garden *H. robustus* blooms at intervals from June through September. The large flowers, often more than three inches long, are as crystalline and as transparently sheer as our atamasco lilies, which they very much resemble, and they look so sweet that it is hard to believe that they are scentless. The petals are white, shading off to rosolane pink at the tips, and to bright green at the throat. It seems odd to call this species robust when the flower is so beautifully fragile, but the name, I gather, refers to the way in which it grows and blooms so freely, and multiplies by seeds and offsets. I have found that it blooms best in a moist, rich soil which contains humus in the form of old manure (leaf-mold is also recommended).

H. brachyandrus is a similar species, except that the flowers are larger (nearly four inches long) and have the bad habit of never opening wide. The petals are a Bourdeaux red at the base, gradually changing to tourmaline pink at the tips. The base shines as if varnished. The whole appears so cool and sparkling that it seems unbelievable that it could appear out of doors in the midsummer heat. This species usually flowers without leaves or with the foliage tips just above the earth. It was discovered in 1888 by Perodi along the banks of the Paraná River. When it first appeared in the trade, it was advertised as hardy only in the Far South, but I have discovered that fainthearted gardeners have little variety in the garden. So, when fall came, I bravely left the expensive bulb in the ground. It has bloomed now, in June and July, for seven summers.

Zephyranthes

The zephyr lilies, flowers of the West Wind, are native to the southern part of this country as well as to Mexico, South America, and the West Indies. Our own atamasco lily is the type species. It has been known to British gardeners since Elizabethan times, when Parkinson called it the Virginia narcissus. Mrs. Loudon says that this species and Z. *candida* are as hardy as the common crocus. I rather doubt that, but Z. *candida* is said to winter as far north as New York, and to be hardy in Tulsa, Oklahoma; and Z. *atamasco* in Pensylvania, New York, and New Jersey.

The atamasco lily, Z. *atamasco*, is native from Virginia to northern Florida and Mississippi and grows in low, wet meadows. It is the first to bloom, coming in April (or sometimes at the end of March), and blooming for six weeks, with an occasional repeater in the summer or fall. In damp, rich soil the pure white lilies are very large and handsome. I have measured specimens with petals three inches and stems twelve inches long. This is one of the few fragrant species.

There are two Florida species. Z. *treatiae* was discovered in 1876 by Mrs. Mary Treat who found it on the banks of a creek. It was named for her by the Harvard professor who pronounced it a new species. I have often wondered why Mrs. Treat, having found this southern flower, sent it up North to be identified. It grows in low pine woods in acid soil, and is said to be difficult in gardens, but has bloomed here for many years, about a month later than our atamasco lily. The buds are red, but the effect of the open flower is pure white. Z. *simpsoni*, the other Florida species, was sent to me for trial by the Amaryllis Society. It bloomed for two seasons at the end of April, and then disappeared. I thought that this was because I had it in too dry and poor a soil. Mr. Hayward says that he finds good drainage one of the main factors in the cultivation of zephyranthes, but I have found just the opposite to be true. I started out with most of the species in very dry soil in a raised bed, and found that those in a very low spot in heavy clay bloomed much better. The buds of *Z. simpsoni* are pink and white striped, and the flowers are even less flaring than those of *Z. treatiae.* All three of these southeastern species require a very acid soil, particularly the Florida ones.

From the Southwest I have had two yellow-flowered species, *Z. longifolia* and *Z. pulchella.* The first came from Mr. Ainsley many years ago, and never bloomed. After some time it disappeared altogether. This is not strange, as I did not know that it requires an alkaline soil. *Z. pulchella* bloomed once, in September, but did not persist. The flower was slightly fragrant, light cadmium yellow, and of short duration.

The best known of all zephyr lilies is *Z. grandiflora,* which we used to know as *Z. carinata,* and which has often been confused with *Z. rosea.* From southern Mexico and Guatemala, it was brought to England from Mexico by Mr. Bullock, in 1825. It is grown in gardens from Virginia and Kentucky to southern Florida, in the Gulf States and California, and naturalized in parts of the South where it "may be found blooming in long-abandoned plantation and country gardens." Here it blooms in the summer, usually in June, but sometimes not until July, and there are repeats in August and September. Margaret Foster Kane wrote in *Herbertia*, 1945, that it blooms in San Antonio, Texas "after every rain beginning in May and continuing until December, often blooming on Christmas Day." The long buds are hellebore red. They open into very wide flat flowers of a deep rose color, "luscious as a bowl of raspberry sherbet," Mr. Hayward says, and I can just see him reaching for a spoon on a hot day. The petals are three and a quarter inches long, and the stems seven inches. The shiny leaves are persistent. This species increases rapidly from offsets, but seldom, if at all, from seed. It is said to do equally well in acid or alkaline soils. *Z. grandiflora* has survived mild winters in Pennsylvania,[2] but in cold climates it is better to lift the bulbs and store them.

Two other Mexican rain lilies have survived Charlotte winters with enough vitality left for flowering in summer. Perhaps because of its tenderness, or supposed tenderness, *Z. macrosiphon* has remained practically unknown to gardeners although it has been in cultivation since the latter part of the nineteenth century. This is too bad, for the fuchsia-purple flowers are small, delicate, and arrogant enough to take their place in those reaches of the rock garden which are reserved for the patricians. At present I have only two bulbs of *Z. mac-*

[2] *Herbertia*, Vol. 3, p. 139.

rosiphon. They bloom in unison, and it is at once ridiculous and mysterious to see twin buds bob up after a wetting. This intriguing event occurs at intervals from early June through September.

Z. *verecunda,* a species from the highlands of central Mexico, has lived outdoors for three years, and since one of the winters was unusually severe I think it may be considered hardy. It blooms sparingly in June, producing a white flower with a fresh green center. There are other forms with flowers described as apple blossom and deep pink. The few pale, narrow leaves come along with the flowers. I have only one bulb, which shows no sign of increase. Planted in quantity this might be an effective species.

Two South American rain lilies are in cultivation in this country. The white swamp lily, Z. *candida,* has been called the hardiest of all species, and is common in gardens from Virginia to Florida, although Mr. Hayward says it is not happy in Florida unless it is given constant care. It is supposed to have been discovered by Juan Diaz de Solis in 1515, near Buenos Aires, where it so whitened the marshes that he gave the La Plata—silver river—its name, "on account of the profusion of white blossoms on the shore." This species will grow in any soil and situation, and will bloom even in dry shade, but it blooms best where there is plenty of moisture. In a low, damp place it blooms all summer and well into the fall. In less ideal circumstances it flowers in August and September. This is one of the little bulbs that travels from garden to garden, and I always like to remember that mine came, along with a choice jonquil, from Mrs. Lay. The flowers are like white crocuses, and the evergreen foliage is rushlike. Mr. Herbert says that he had "seventy flowers expanded at once on a small patch of this plant at Spofforth," and that the leaves "resist the severest frost of our usual winters." This is another little bulb that blooms in California and the Gulf States as well as in the Southeast.

Z. *citrina* is like a sweet-scented lemon-colored crocus, except that the small flowers are held on very tall stems. Once established in moist soil, it blooms once a month all summer, from June or July to September or October. From *Herbertia* contributors I gather that it does well in Winter Park, San Antonio, and Wichita Falls; but it was not long-lived in Raleigh, and has not been a success in Charlotte. It may need lime.

The only hybrid zephyr lily is Z. *ajax,* a cross between Z. *candida* and Z. *citrina.* The leaves are round, and the tall-stemmed croeuslike flowers are a sparkling citron yellow. It blooms at any time from late June to early October. "It is a very free bloomer and rapid multiplier both by offset and seed," Mrs. Strout writes from California, "and it grows well in a lime soil and also a neutral one." For me it grows well in an acid soil.

I have tried to grow several of the brilliant and exquisite zephyranthes of the West Indies but none of them have persisted, and only two have bloomed or even lived through a winter. Even when planted in the spring they are not certain to bloom that season. Since the life of a bulb from the tropics is affected by so many more factors than low temperature, it is hard to make up one's mind to give up trying to grow them out of doors.

Z. rosea, Mrs. Loudon says, "was found at the Havannah by Mr. George Don, and introduced by him in 1823." This tiny and beautiful flower from the mountains of Cuba thrives in Winter Park and near San Francisco, but so far not in North Carolina. For a long time I had trouble getting the right bulb, for the *Z. rosea* of the trade often proves to be *Z. grandiflora*. But at last I got the true species, planted it late in December, and it flowered the following August and again in September. For a few years afterward, leaves appeared but no flowers, and then it disappeared altogether. I have tried it a number of times since, but there has never been another blossom. I remember the flowers as being exquisitely proportioned and of a wonderful rose color, but I had no Ridgway chart in those days, and so I cannot describe it exactly. The petals were a little over an inch long, and the stems only two inches and a half.

Z. tubispatha was sent to me by Mr. Hayward with the warning that it would probably not be hardy, and he was right. Gardeners in Florida love to tell gardeners in North Carolina that plants will not be hardy. Mrs. Loudon had this to say: "The species is a native of the Blue Mountains in Jamaica, and it is too tender to bear the open air in England." But Miss Kell said, in *Herbertia*,[3] that she grows it on the Texas plains, and "the lovely little flowers bloom during a very long season." Mrs. Loudon described the "elegantly shaped" flowers as white with a green base, and never opening very wide.

Z. insularum, which flourishes in Florida and California, lived in my gardens for several years, and bloomed in the summer in a half-hearted manner, but I think that both plantings have now disappeared. The flowers are white with a green throat and a red stain on the outside. It bloomed beside the globe daisy, *Globularia bellidifolia,* and the tiny white zephyr lily was in perfect harmony with the ball-like blue flowers, but before long the globularia was gone, too. This zephyr lily blooms in gardens in Key West and in Cuba, but it has never been found in the wild.

Z. bifolia, which came to me as *Habranthus cardinalis,* is a native of San Domingo, and this also is too tender "to bear the open air" in North Carolina. Mr. Hayward says that the graceful, nodding flowers are of a most delectable tint of salmon-red. He adds that it "grows well in the coral soil of the Bahamas, but wastes away after a few years in Florida, possibly because of lack of lime."

And so you see there are zephyr lilies for every part of the South, but it may take a little experimenting to find which ones do best for you.

[3] Vol. 3, 1945, p. 134.

Some Amaryllids

Cooperia

Joseph Cooper was gardener to the Earl Fitzwilliam at Wentworth House, England. When the bulbs of this amaryllid, sent out from Texas by Mr. Drummond, flowered in the earl's collection, Mr. Herbert named them, not for the nobleman, but for the man who brought them to bloom. Cooperia, the last of the three groups of little bulbs known to me as rain lilies, actually is the only one so listed in many references. Drummond's cooperia, or evening star, *C. drummondi,* with its very long red tube and small white flower, was thought "more curious than beautiful." The green-tubed variety *C. d. chlorosolen,* also called evening star and described as having the fragrance of a primrose, was sent to England at the same time, in 1834. Nowadays this species is considered of little garden value, but I have always been sorry that it would not bloom for me, for a flower whose "heavy perfume attracts large moths" must have some charm in the eye of the beholder. It should be valuable for its season of bloom, too; it comes into flower at the end of summer when the rains come to the prairies after the long drought.

The beautiful Texas prairie lily, *C. pedunculata,* blooms in spring and summer, from April to July, and occasionally in August. Like the evening star, it comes out at twilight, and the incomparable chalk-white flowers scent the night. They smell like all the perfumes of

Araby. The firm, round bulbs have very long necks and need to be planted four inches deep in alkaline soil. They are found in part shade, but bloom for me only in the open. This is one of the most easily grown of the small amaryllids for all parts of the South, and is hardy at least as far north as Virginia and Oklahoma. Farther north the bulbs can be lifted in fall and stored until spring. My first bulbs came to me years ago from the Rev. C. W. Hall. There were twenty of them, and I was glad to have so many for they increased little, if any, in more than ten years, although they bloomed better with every season. Mr. Hall wrote that they were found in low, moist places, but more adapted to well-drained soil. Since the foliage is scant and inconspicuous, the bulbs can be tucked in among low spring-flowering plants to give a second season's bloom in the same spot. It seems strange that these beautiful flowers, which give so much and demand so little and have been in cultivation for more than a hundred years, should still be so little known outside of their provenance. Shortly after heavy rains in spring and early summer, lawns, meadows, and woods in Louisiana, Texas, and Mexico are covered with them.

C. brasiliensis came from Mr. Mulford Foster who collected it in Brazil in 1939. The bulbs have come through two of the most trying winters in Charlotte and bloomed in June and July for several seasons. Dr. Traub reports that they bloomed at intervals from spring until fall in Salinas, California, and that they are satisfactory in pots in colder climates. The flowers are as white and as fragrant as, but smaller than, those of the prairie lily, and have taller, more slender stems.

The most delightful of all the rain lilies I have had came from Texas as *Allium nuttalli,* but must have been a cooperia. The bulbs had been collected for Miss Kell in the Davis Mountains near Fort Stockton. They were planted in February, and in July a bud suddenly appeared with no foliage (that came later, a slender strand or two). The bud quickly opened into a small white flower, as carefully wrought as a cyclamen or a miniature daffodil, and innocent of any aspect of the onion. Miss Kell wrote me later that her own bulbs failed to bloom and did not survive a north Texas winter. The next year we left Raleigh, and I had to leave behind this perfect little flower without even being certain of its name.

Twenty years ago, when cooperias first came into my garden, no yellow-flowered species were known. Since then two have been discovered, *C. smalli,* which is beginning to creep into the lists of rare bulb dealers, and *C. jonesi,* which is still in the hands of collectors. They are found growing together in southern Texas. *C. smalli* blooms in June in Florida, in July in Texas, and in September in North Carolina, but everywhere keeps its habit of opening early in the afternoon rather than at dusk. The flowers are not so minute as those of Miss Kell's little bulb, but the crisp petals and shallow cup of chrome yellow and the neat column of ivory stamens are fashioned with the same finesse. Characteristically tall stems (eight inches) give them an air of standing on tiptoe. The tiny bulb can be tucked into a rock crevice, or among other small flowers, where it takes up practically no space, and is unobtrusive until it suddenly bursts into bloom. The only lack in the yellow cooperias is that they are scentless—or nearly so.

Several years ago Dr. Flory sent me, in a collection of rain lilies, a cross between *Cooperia brasiliensis* and *C. drummondi chlorosolen,* which still lives but has never bloomed. In the same collection there was another interesting hybrid, called cooperanthes (cooperia X zephyranthes). In 1936 Mr. Sydney Percy-Lancaster sent the American Amaryllis Society a hundred named hybrids of this cross, from his collection in India. "Originally," he wrote, "the shades of colour were white, pinks, and yellows. Then combinations between pinks and yellows became possible, and some lovely orange and salmon shades have come about." [4] My bulb, after slumbering for two years, suddenly blossomed forth one July. The scentless flower has the smooth texture of a cooperia and the crocuslike form of *Zephyranthes citrina,* but the color, a cool luminous yellow, is all its own. It opens at noon, as a compromise between the morning and evening habits of its parents, and never opens very wide.

[4] *Herbertia,* Vol. 3, 1936, p. 109.

11

Little Bulbs in Pots

Winter-flowering little bulbs bloom indoors almost from the time the cold of winter takes the color from the garden until the spring sunshine puts it back again. Getting the bulbs ready for forcing should be considered part of autumn's round of chores. The little ones are the best of house plants for they fit into pots small enough for a window ledge, and they are easily managed and long in bloom. Since most of them are cheap enough to discard after flowering, they need window space only when in bud and in bloom. During that time their only requirements are a cool room, not over seventy by day not under thirty-five at night, and the sun afforded by a south or east window.

Bulbs to be forced are best planted as soon as they are available, usually September and October, for the longer they are kept out in the air the less vigorous they will be. It is better to regulate the succession of bloom by scheduling the times that the pots are to be brought in to light and heat, rather than by spacing the times of planting.

Pots must be clean, and new ones soaked in water for a day or two before they are filled. A concave stone or fragment of broken pot goes over the drainage hole, then an inch of pebbles for a small pot and two inches for a large one; a layer of damp sphagnum over the pebbles keeps them clear of soil. Another layer on top of the filled pot keeps the soil from drying out. The peat is all the better for having some pulverized leaf-mold mixed with it. A little cow manure can go in, too, if it is old enough to powder, but Mr. Houdyshel prefers a tablespoon of bonemeal and a teaspoon of blood-meal to every six-inch pot of soil. Commercial fiber does as well as the peat and sand mixture as a potting medium, is cleaner, and saves all of this trouble.

The pots should be large enough so that the bulbs may be planted with ample soil beneath and an inch or two above them. Bulbs in pots need shallower planting than those in gardens. Water them thoroughly but gently, and then let the pots drain before storing. From three to five small bulbs—or even eight to twelve of the very small ones—are right for a five- or six-inch pot.

For successful bloom the pots must be left in a cool, dark place until the bulbs are well rooted. Pots of hardy bulbs can be sunk in the open ground as soon as they are planted, and left for two months (six weeks may do, if you can't wait), or until they are wanted. Cover the pots with a layer of sand, then a layer of soil, then a thick layer of leaves or litter. When the pots are brought indoors, they must first go into a cool store-room or light basement, and then introduced gradually to light, warmth, and water before they are put in direct sunlight. When fully in bloom, the flowers will last longer with some shade.

All sorts of small hardy bulbs can be grown indoors, although some do better than others. Spring-flowering crocuses are good; the named varieties make the most show—if a big show is what is wanted. They force quickly, needing only six or seven weeks for rooting. They should be left in the dark until the tops are about an inch high, and the flowers should be kept in a cool place away from the afternoon sun. The fall-flowering kinds can be potted and set directly in the window without any rooting period at all. Perhaps this is the best way to grow the late and fragile species, too, for no matter how lovely they are out of doors, some of the blooms will be frosted. Grape hyacinths do well in pots, especially the one called Early Giant. Snowdrops are good if the room is cool enough. Allow eight bulbs to a five-inch pot. Scillas, puschkinias, and chionodoxas bloom indoors, and *Iris reticulata* is a window-garden favorite. Six of the little netted bulbs of the iris will fit into a four-inch pot. If planted in October they will bloom for Christmas or soon afterward.

Half-hardy bulbs intended for winter flowering indoors must be potted up and left to root in a cool, dark, airy place (not a closed closet). The rooting place should never go higher than forty to forty-five degrees, but the cooler the better (as long as they do not freeze). Water them once when they are planted, and keep them barely moist until they are well rooted. When top growth starts, bring them into a lighter and slightly warmer place for about a week, increasing the water supply gradually.

Of the small winter-flowering members of the iris family, the freesias, babianas, and sparaxis are best for window gardens. The delicate tints and heavy fragrance of the freesias and babianas, and the brilliant red and gold of sparaxis, bring to the indoor garden all of the extravagance of spring. Since the tops and roots of the bulbs start at the same time, they are an exception to the general bulb-forcing rule and do not need to be kept in the dark at all. As soon as growth starts they must have plenty of water. All require full sun, air, and a cool room—not over sixty-five degrees for the best results; they will not bloom if it is much warmer. Top-size freesia bulbs, from a half-inch to an inch in diameter, grow best and bloom best. They cost so little more than lesser grades that it is better to have a few of them than more of a smaller size. Bulbs planted early in the fall sometimes bloom for Christmas. They can be planted later to lengthen the season, even through November, although the late ones will have short stems. Six large bulbs of freesia or sparaxis are enough for a five-inch pot. They need an inch of soil for covering. Perhaps twice as many babianas can go into a pot of the same size, but even though the bulbs are the smallest of the group, they must be planted two inches deep. Babianas and sparaxis are not very well known, but they should be, for they are more easily grown than freesias.

Most of the small amaryllids are summer-flowering, but some of the cyrtanthus bloom in pots in winter. Those that I have had grew in the garden, and it is difficult to find specific directions for pot culture, for each species differs in habits and requirements, and what will do for one will not suit another. In *Herbertia*, 1937, Mr. Ruckman gives his method for growing three kinds: *Cyrtanthus mackeni* (which blooms in late winter), and two others of uncertain identity. "How such choice and easily-handled bulbs as cyrtanthus can have been neglected so long is a mystery. The only trouble seems to be to get the bulbs in the first place. The bulbs are small and should be potted up singly in three-inch pots in the soil mixture used for hybrid amaryllis, with the upper quarter of the bulb above ground. They start into growth in November and bloom during

January and February. After blooming a strong growth should be encouraged until the foliage ripens, usually about the middle of June. From then until November they should be kept dry or nearly so, as are other deciduous amaryllids when in their dormant state. The bulbs form offsets rather freely and these should be kept growing with the old bulb until the pot becomes badly crowded, as is the practice with vallota, the Scarborough lily. Occasional waterings with liquid manure both before and after blooming are beneficial. A little of the old surface soil may be removed from the pots and replaced with fresh just before growth begins."

The aforementioned soil mixture for hybrid amaryllis is made up of good loam and sand with equal parts of powdered leafmold and old manure. Other species that have been grown in pots are *C. ochroleucus*, which blooms indoors in February, and *C. parviflorus*, in early spring.

Nerine filifolia is particularly valuable for its blooming season, October to December. Since the foliage is evergreen the bulbs are sent at any season, but spring is the time to pot them for they travel better then, and are more easily established. They can be had in late summer in bud, which is a temptation, but if my experience is any guide it is a lure to be avoided. The bulbs should be planted with the soil up only to their necks, six to a six-inch pot.

There are several window-garden favorites in the lily family, among them the colorful Cape cowslips. These should be potted in August and September for late winter bloom, and never later than October. The golden *Lachenalia aurea* and the coral *L. pendula superba* sometimes bloom for Christmas. The later-flowering *L. tricolor* is most amenable in pots, and the most frequently offered. Plant six in a six-inch pot, and cover with only half an inch of soil.

Mr. Houdyshel considers *Allium triquetrum* the most effective species for pots, even better than the more commonly-grown Naples onion. I have had it only in the garden, and I do not know when it blooms indoors, or how well it looks. However, it is one of the best alliums for use as seasoning, and might find a place on the kitchen window sill if that is not too intimate a place for a plant so strongly scented. *A. neapolitanum* has the advantage of being entirely without the garlic odor, and in the variety *grandiflorum* it is a striking plant. Put from three to five bulbs in a five-inch pot, and cover with an inch of soil.

Another *Herbertia* [1] entry offers the information that, "as a double-duty bulb, *Brodiaea uniflora* is priceless because it forces easily. If it is potted in late October one has the cheery blue stars week after week, through November to January. All that is necessary is to pot the corms (six to a four-inch pot) in a good soil mixture and water regularly. A sunny window is the best. There are no requirements for rooting in the dark, or for storage or for growing temperatures other than those of the

[1] Vol. 10, p. 165.

ordinary living room. In order to prolong the blooming period into February and March, a few dormant corms saved for the purpose are added to each pot in January in spaces left for them. In April or May the growing plants should be lifted and planted outdoors to make their full growth and then to remain dormant until it is time to lift them again for potting."

Where the weather is too severe to have them out of doors, the winter-flowering hoopskirts do well in pots, and even where the bulbs are hardy some gardeners prefer to grow them indoors. Their early flowering makes them especially desirable. In the *Rock Garden Bulletin* for January, 1955 (p. 15), Mr. Harold Epstein deals with *Narcissus bulbocodium monophyllus* and the varieties *foliosus* and *romieuxi*: "The ideal growing conditions are in pots in a cool greenhouse (temperature not lower than forty-five degrees F.) where they usually come into bloom here (Larchmont, New York) in mid-November and generally last to the end of the year. They must be fully ripened and allowed to be well baked and dry through the summer. They can also be cultivated in coldframes under glass sash and when ready to bloom they are brought indoors preferably into a light cool room. Under such cool conditions the flowers with their protruding style and golden anthers will be long-lasting. My bulbs have been in the same soil for the third season but will be transplanted when dormant during the coming year."

I have planted achimenes in the garden a number of

times, but without much success. Tubers of the common kind, the rather dull, dark, violet-flowered one, generally bloom from the end of August into October if they are planted in April. Tubers left in the ground never bloomed the second year, although they are said to be hardy to Washington, D.C. In Charlotte, Mrs. Whisnant has very good success with the ones that she pots in spring and grows on the terrace. Out of doors they must have shade and plenty of water. As house plants they are fairly demanding, too. Mr. Houdyshel says that they do not bloom well in parts of California where the nights are cool: "The name is said to mean that they do not like the cold. This may be fanciful but is nevertheless true. They like warm days and nights. [Thus their wide acceptance as house plants.] A good temperature will not be under sixty at night and up to eighty daytimes, and higher will not hurt them. Pot the tubers in a horizontal position and cover with about an inch of soil. We mulch the surface with a thin layer of sphagnum moss to prevent erosion when watering. Keep them only a little moist until growth is started. When growing well, keep them wet." An occasional watering with liquid manure is advisable. From one to five tubers can be grown in a five-inch pot, but Mr. Houdyshel recommends ten-inch baskets, lined with sphagnum and filled with fibrous peat or peat and coarse leafmold in equal parts. Gradually decrease watering after flowering ceases. When the foliage has died away the pots can be laid on their sides and stored dry, in a place where the temperature does not go below fifty degrees.

Finally, there are the winter-flowering wood sorrels (oxalis). These are perhaps the easiest of all the little bulbs to grow in pots, and one of the most satisfactory, for they are long in bloom. Plant the bulbs two inches deep, three to a five-inch pot if they are large, and twice as many if they are small. Wood sorrels can be shipped as late as the middle of October, but since they may begin to sprout in August they should be ordered early. Any soil will do, although a rich mixture is appreciated. A cool room and full sun are necessities. The bulbs do not need to be started in the dark, so the pots can be put into the window at once. The tuberous-rooted sorts start slowly. In the summer the pots can be taken out of doors and laid on their sides to dry off. The bulbs will bloom year after year.

Three bulbs of the fall-flowering *Oxalis bowieana* can be planted in a five-inch pot. This is another of the little bulbs to be grown outdoors in summer, indoors in winter in all but frost-free areas. The bulbs must not be forgotten in the rush of fall chores, for they may be caught by early frosts if they are left in the garden. Also good is the buttercup-yellow *O. cernua,* called Bermuda buttercup. It comes from South Africa, but is naturalized in Bermuda and Florida. There is also a double-flowered form that makes a smaller plant.

O. crassipes is evergreen and ever-blooming. After it has done its duty in the garden in the summer, it can be brought into the house to bloom in winter. The Grand

Duchess is probably a form of *O. variabilis*, so called because the flowers vary from rose to purple to white. As I know them they are a lovely clear pink, a color I have never seen in other species. They are very large, too, and stand well above the low leaves.

O. hirta is different from the other species in that the plants are trailing and the leaflets narrow. It blooms late in the fall and is one of the tender sorts. Because the stems hang down, this is a good plant for hanging baskets or a wall bracket. A single bulb will do for a four-inch pot. Unlike the other species, this one will bloom in part shade, and even opens its glowing flowers on gloomy days.

12

Sources of Bulbs

The most valuable information a garden book has to offer is the names of plantsmen who supply the material described, for that is all the reader really needs to know. Once he has the plants he can discover the rest for himself. When the subject is little bulbs, a list of sources is all the more valuable. Well-known bulbs are offered by well-known growers or importers, but the little-known and rare bulbs are mostly offered by specialists who seldom advertise and who must be persistently pursued. "I hide myself from the general public and have no signs," Mr. Heath wrote me with great satisfaction. "It takes a real enthusiast to find me. Only yesterday a couple from Pittsburgh spent three hours hunting my place."

When you request a price list from these collectors, do not expect a handsomely illustrated catalogue. They "need not praise who purpose not to sell." The poorer the pages and the print, the rarer the bulbs probably will be. Do not give away your copy of a catalogue or brochure to a fellow gardener, or drop it in the scrap basket upon the receipt of another. Preserve all such publications, for they are extremely limited editions, and each one is likely to contain some invaluable information not to be found elsewhere.

Among the treasures of my garden library is a set of Mr. Houdyshel's brochures, sent out every spring and fall for the last twenty years. In each issue he has let fall some word of wisdom left out of the others. And, as gardeners go from enthusiasm to enthusiasm, some issues contain more about rain lilies and others more about brodiaeas, but the lot of them proffer more practical advice on more kinds of bulbs than any book that I have ever read. I often wonder how many people have availed themselves of this knowledge that is the result of a life's labor and is theirs for the asking.

One of the best places to seek rare bulbs is in the bulletins circulated free of charge by some state departments of agriculture. My favorite is the *Mississippi*

Market Bulletin (published in Jackson) which has come to me ever since Eudora Welty put my name on the mailing list many years ago. Here you will find rain lilies, oxalis, jonquils, achimines, snowdrops, and white summer crocuses—for small sums or in exchange for printed feed bags; but you must remember that the snowdrops will be snowflakes, and that the crocus will be *Zephyranthes candida*. Some of the names in the lists are more picturesque than accurate, and I have to order the bulbs to satisfy my curiosity. I would be willing to wager that the "polly comb bulbs" offered recently will prove to be *Alstroemeria pulchella*, which is sometimes called parrot flower.

Once when I asked Mr. Hayward how to go about getting plants not in the nurseries, he replied: "Write to botanical gardens, and get in touch with missionaries and army officers in all parts of the world." I had always thought that botanical gardens spoke only to other botanical gardens, or perhaps to a few individuals high up in the horticultural world, but thus encouraged I wrote boldly to the New York Botanical Garden, asking for a source for *Laucojum autumnale*. My answer was a gift of the very bulbs themselves. Now, I understand, the Garden sends out to members a list of bulbs for sale. Another source of supply is the seed exchange of the American Rock Garden Society.

Sometimes, I find, you do not have to make an effort to find rare plants. They turn up of themselves. Once when I was in despair of ever getting one of the little daffodils, I found it in the mail one morning. Another time I found that a crocus I was seeking had been growing for some time in my own garden. Since it had never bloomed, I did not know that it was the one I was looking for. Therefore, I no longer make it a point of honor never to mention a plant without being able to name a source for it. Any day it may turn up. To seek is to find—maybe the thing sought is already possessed—and sometimes seeking is an end in itself.

Carroll Gardens
444 E. Main Street
Westminster, Maryland
    21157

The Daffodil Mart
Rt. 3, Box 208R
Gloucester, Virginia 23061

DeJager Bulbs
188 Asbury St.
S. Hamilton, Massachu-
    setts 01981

Dutch Gardens, Inc.
P.O. Box 400
Montvale, New Jersey
    07645

International Grower's
    Exchange
Box 397
Farmington, Michigan
    48024

McClure & Zimmerman
1422 West Thorndale
Chicago, Illinois 60660

Messelaar Bulb Co.
County Rd., Rt. 1A, Box
    269
Ipswich, Massachusetts
    01938

Montrose Nursery
P.O. Box 957
Hillsborough, North
    Carolina 27278

Park Seed Co.
Greenwood, South Caro-
lina 29647

White Flower Farm
Litchfield, Connecticut
06759

Anthony J. Skittone
2271 31st Ave.
San Francisco, California
94116

For the Armchair Gardener

Aiken, George D., *Pioneering with Wild Flowers* (Putney, Vermont, 1933).

Bowles, Edward A., *A Handbook of Crocus and Colchicum* (New York, Van Nostrand, 1952).

Brown, M. J. Jefferson, *The Daffodil, Its History, Varieties, and Cultivation* (London, 1951).

Carleton, R., *Hardy Bulbs* (New York, Rinehart, 1955).

Cave, Norman Leslie, *The Iris* (New York, Chanticleer Press, 1951).

Dormon, Caroline, *Wild Flowers of Louisiana* (New York, Doubleday, 1934).

Everett, Thomas Henry, *The American Gardener's Book of Bulbs* (New York, Random House, 1954).

Gray, Alec, *Miniature Daffodils* (New York, Transatlantic Arts, 1955).

Hall, Sir Alfred Daniel, *The Book of the Tulip* (London, 1929).

Jacob, Rev. Joseph, *Hardy Bulbs for Amateurs* (London, 1924).

———, *Tulips* (New York, F. A. Stokes, 1912).

Loudon, Mrs., *The Ladies Flower Garden of Ornamental Bulbus Plants* (London, n.d.).

McFarland, J. Horace, *Garden Bulbs in Color* (New York, Macmillan, 1938).

McKinney, Ella Porter, *Iris in the Little Garden* (Boston, Little, Brown, 1927).

Norton, Claire, *How To Grow Spring Flowers From Bulbs* (New York, Doubleday, 1935).

Peters, Ruth Marie, *Bulb Magic for Your Window* (New York, M. Barrows, 1954).

Rockwell, Frederick F., *The Complete Book of Bulbs* (New York, Doubleday, 1953).

Synge, Patric M., *Flowers in Winter* (London, 1948).

Weathers, John, *The Bulb Book* (New York, E. P. Dutton, 1911).

Wilder, Louis Beebe, *Pleasures and Problems of a Rock Garden* (New York, Garden City, 1937).

Wister, J. C., *Bulbs for American Gardens* (Boston, The Stratford Co., 1930).

———, *The Iris* (London, 1927).

PERIODICALS

Alpine Garden Society Bulletin Secretary, Lye End Link, St. John's, Woking, Surrey GU21 1SW.

American Rock Garden Society Bulletin Buffy Parker, 15 Fairmead Road, Darien, Connecticut 06820.

Index

Index

Index

Index

Index

Library of Congress Cataloging-in-Publication Data
Lawrence, Elizabeth.
The little bulbs.

Reprint. Originally published: New York : Criterion
Books, 1957.
Bibliography: p.
Includes index.
1. Bulbs.   I. Title.
SB425.L3   1986   635.9′44   85-29399
ISBN 0-8223-0739-1 (pbk.)